CONDUCTING INTERPRETIVE POLICY ANALYSIS

DVORA YANOW

Qualitative Research Methods
Volume 47

Sage Publications
International Educational and Professional Publisher
Thousand Oaks   London   New Delhi

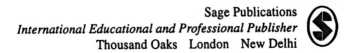

For information:

 Sage Publications, Inc.
2455 Teller Road
Thousand Oaks, California 91320
E-mail: order@sagepub.com

Sage Publications Ltd.
6 Bonhill Street
London EC2A 4PU
United Kingdom

Sage Publications India Pvt. Ltd.
M-32 Market
Greater Kailash I
New Delhi 110 048 India

Printed in the United States of America

Library of Congress Cataloging-in-Publication Data

Main entry under title:

Yanow, Dvora.
   Conducting interpretive policy analysis / by Dvora Yanow.
   p. cm. — (Qualitative research methods ; v. 47)
   Includes bibliographical references.
   ISBN 978-0-7619-0826-5
   ISBN 978-0-7619-0827-2
   1. Policy sciences. I. Title. II. Series.
   H97.Y368 1999
   320'.6—dc21   99-6588

            09 10 6 5 4 3

Acquiring Editor:	Peter Labella
Editorial Assistant:	Renée Piernot
Production Editor:	Denise Santoyo
Production Assistant:	Nevair Kabakian
Typesetter:	Danielle Dillahunt

CONTENTS

SERIES EDITORS' INTRODUCTION

Policy analysis generally concerns the needs for, and the proper nature of, actions taken by authority—a federal agency, local government, a business firm, a hospital, a non-governmental organization—to achieve executive goals. Over the second half of this century, the practice of policy analysis has emphasized in particular the quantitative comparison of policy costs and benefits. The standard procedure begins with a specification of philosophy, objectives and the situation at hand. The analyst then marshals information to evaluate the (dis)advantages of alternative courses of action. The analysis culminates with a recommendation and, in some instances, a plan of implementation.

In *Conducting Interpretive Policy Analysis,* Dvora Yanow introduces a qualitative complement to the quantitive family of policy analytical techniques. Rather than asking the question "What are the costs of a policy?" the practitioner of interpretive policy analysis asks instead "What are the meanings of a policy?"

Yanow's book builds from the premise that the promise and implications of a policy are not transparent and easily evident in its text. Instead they are hidden (and sometimes incompatible) conclusions that are warranted in different ways by the assumptions of policymakers and multiple constituencies. To unwrap these perspectives, the interpretive policy analyst must identify groups of stakeholders and the "policy artifacts" (consisting of symbolic language, objects, and actions) that determine how a policy, together with the policy process, is "framed" or understood.

Yanow's volume—the forty-seventh of Sage's **Qualitative Research Methods Series**—informs how the "architecture of meaning" is revealed by the systematic investigation of policy categories and labels, metaphors and narratives, programs and institutional places. With this contribution, policy analysis is shown to involve not only decisions, dollars, and scientific facts, but also rituals and mythologies. The book should be a useful policy companion to qualitative policy manuals.

—Marc L. Miller
John Van Maanen
Peter K. Manning

PREFACE

Imagine, in the following fictionalized account, that you are a policy analyst working for the mayor of Oakland, California. It is the late fall of 1996. The head of the School Committee has just brought the mayor the final draft of their report on students' performance on standardized tests. It indicates that, of the entire student population, African Americans have consistently, over time, tested in the lowest ranks. The School Committee's recommendations include applying for municipal, federal, and private teacher-training funds to establish a new program to train teachers in the use of "Ebonics," a name for the form of English spoken by many African American children in the school system (and elsewhere in the United States), to help students improve their performance. The Committee wants the mayor's public endorsement of this proposal, thinking that this will strengthen their application to the City Council and to other funding sources. Perhaps they can even use the mayor's support to attract news coverage and public attention. The mayor calls you in, hands you the proposal, and asks for your analysis of it as a policy matter. How do you proceed?

If you were trained in traditional policy analysis, you might do a cost-benefit analysis of the proposed teacher-training program. You might discover that other school districts have instituted similar programs and conduct a comparative analysis of test scores and costs across all or a sample of sites. If you were particularly oriented toward citizen participation, you might initiate a survey of parents or of taxpayers (to the extent that the latter is a more inclusive category), or even of teachers, to get their opinions. Your report to the mayor would either recommend that she endorse the proposal and allocate funds to the program or not, based on an "objective" assessment of its anticipated costs and benefits. Or, if your research discovers that the choice (to endorse or not to endorse) raises complex subsequent choices, you might present your analysis as a path diagram analyzing the various options and their consequences.

If you were trained in interpretive techniques, however, you would be more likely to proceed differently, beginning with the questions, What does this proposed program mean; and, For whom does it have meaning? You would anticipate that the program would mean different things to different school system constituencies, and your first step would then be to begin identifying those different communities of meaning, so that you could find out what Ebonics (or an Ebonics teacher-training program) means for each group. You might begin by interviewing the members of the School Committee to see what they had in mind in proposing the program, and then interview teachers, students, parents, and other stakeholders you identify during your research. You might discover, in this process, that the understandings of the policy issues condensed in the word "Ebonics" are vast, complex, contradictory, and exceedingly emotionally charged, that even within the African American community, meaning is not uniform and the subject is hotly contested. Your report to the mayor, then, would consist of an analysis of the architecture of meaning in the Ebonics issue—that is, the various ways it is being "framed": the details of what it means, for which groups it holds those meanings, and what the conflicting interpretations are. You might recommend that the mayor call a public forum on the matter or take some other form of action to discuss the issues publicly before she decides whether or not to endorse the School Committee's proposal. In framing your recommendation, you would also focus on what meaning or meanings the mayor's act might have for the various policy-relevant groups.

Policy analysis seeks to inform some audience—traditionally, the policymaker—about an anticipated policy: what its impact will be on a target population, whether it is likely to achieve the desired outcome, whether it is the right policy to address a specific problem. Given the facts of human nature and the ambiguity that characterizes human enterprise, including the realm of public policies, anticipated policies can often be cast in alternate forms, and the choice of the best possible form must be made according to some criterion. Under the impact of developments in the late 1960s and 1970s in decision, operations, and statistical analyses, the criterion most commonly put forward for making these choices was a weighing of costs and benefits and their influence on decision points and ensuing choice paths. Under the philosophically-based judgment that values were not an appropriate realm of scientific assessment, nonmonetary costs and benefits were translated into dollar terms for analysis or bracketed and dropped from consideration. As quantitatively-based technical expertise came to dominate the practices of policy analysis and planning, critiques arose (influenced by the political atmosphere of the 1960s and 1970s) calling for more democratic processes, such as advocacy planning (Peattie, 1968) and participatory decision making. Critics also pointed to the limitations of quantifying values, making evaluative criteria explicit, and other issues (see, e.g., Kelly, 1987).

Interpretive forms of policy analysis seek to develop a different approach to this set of issues. Returning to the matter of values—now informed by a different understanding of the place of values in science and by questions regarding the facticity of "facts"—interpretive policy analysis shifts the discussion from values as a set of costs, benefits, and choice points to a focus on values, beliefs, and feelings as a set of meanings, and from a view of human behavior as, ideally, instrumentally and technically rational to human action as expressive (of meaning). Under the sway of thinking in the philosophies of science, social science, and knowledge, especially the work of Thomas Kuhn, Alfred Schutz (often through his followers, Peter Berger and Thomas Luckmann), Charles Taylor, and others, policy theorists have critiqued the underpinnings of positivist-informed analysis and are developing alternative approaches.[1]

In this book I will sketch out, very briefly, the terms of the philosophical debate (in Chapter 1), and then take up some of the varieties of interpretive methods that might be used in policy analysis of various sorts, beginning in Chapter 2 with the identification of interpretive communities.

Both of these areas—the philosophical and the methodological—are vast, and I cannot cover either in depth in this small volume. In particular, because there is so little published to date treating interpretive (or "qualitative") policy analysis, and because existing methods texts on the whole do not link the tools presented to their underlying philosophical presuppositions, I have chosen to focus on the conceptual grounding for the interpretive methods I present, at times at the expense of a more detailed "how-to." I also do not dwell on definitions of public policy, its processes, or its analysis, as I imagine my readers to be students, academics, and professionals who bring such background to this reading. I have attempted to include an extensive set of references, which will lead the interested reader to original texts and their critical treatment, as well as to further sources and more detailed presentations of methods. I present one map—one reading—of this vast terrain.

Let me raise two central cautions here. First, "interpretive" does not mean "impressionistic." Even though interpretive methods emphasize the centrality of human interpretation and, hence, subjective meaning—that is, meaning to the "subject," the actor or the researcher—they are, nonetheless, methods: systematic, rigorous, methodical. But because they rely on human meaning-making, which is of necessity responsive to the highly variable context of the research setting, the steps of these methods typically cannot be set out in as discrete and regularized a fashion as those of cost-benefit, decision, or regression analysis and their counterparts. It is the rhetorical power of the orderly, seemingly finite steps of these latter methods which convey their sense of rigor; conversely, the absence of that rhetoric from interpretive methods implies (to some) their lack of rigor. In practice, interpretive methods are as formal—"conforming to accepted rules or customs" (*Oxford Minidictionary,* 1981, p. 171)—as the more traditional ones, and, conversely, traditional methods entail as much human judgment and interpretation as do interpretive ones.

Second, there has been a tendency in some discussions of symbolic politics to treat that concept as distinct from "real" politics, as if symbols and their meanings were not "real," or as if material redistributions and instrumental actions were the only "real" elements of political and policy acts. The distinction is erroneous and misleading. Policies and political actions are not *either* symbolic or substantive: they can be both at once. Conceptually speaking, even purely instrumental intentions are communicated and apperceived through symbolic means. In practice, policies are intended to achieve something material, or expressive, or both. To do so, they have recourse only to symbolic representations to accomplish their purposes, and these purposes can be understood only by interpretations of those representations. There can be no unmediated, directly apperceived policy or agency actions.

Lastly, if methods based on a positivist ontology (presuppositions about reality) and epistemology (presuppositions about the knowability of that reality) also entail interpretive acts, why call the alternative described here "interpretive"? This language is one of the ways in which methods commonly referred to as "qualitative" are increasingly being designated ("constructivist" being another). It signals and underscores the link between methods and their underlying presuppositions: the ways we go about "collecting" and analyzing data derive from and reflect prior suppositions about the reality status and knowability of the subject of our research. This is also one reason not to call them "qualitative." That term emerged to distinguish a set of field-based, non-statistically-grounded methods from "quantitative" ones; but since "qualitative" (or interpretive) researchers also count, the distinction captured in those terms is increasingly meaningless. The qualitative-quantitative nomenclature is increasingly understood as connoting differences of philosophical presuppositions denoted by the positivist-interpretive distinction. Hence, conducting interpretive policy analysis.

NOTE

1. I have in mind here Kuhn (1962), Schutz (1962), Berger and Luckmann (1966), Taylor (1971), and Ricoeur (1971). See Hawkesworth (1988) for an excellent philosophical critique of the positivist presuppositions of traditional policy analysis.

ACKNOWLEDGMENTS

I am deeply grateful to my colleagues in academia—Ralph Brower, Frank Fischer, Michel van Eeten—and in practice—Peter Plug—as well as series editor John Van Maanen, who offered encouragement and extensive, at times talmudic, commentary on the manuscript. They will find their influences reflected in these pages. Series editor Peter Manning also provided useful foils for shaping the text. I dedicate this volume to the memory of my mother, Helen Vogel Yanow (1921-1998), who was an incisive seeker after methodical, but humanistic, truth.

CONDUCTING INTERPRETIVE POLICY ANALYSIS

DVORA YANOW
California State University, Hayward

1. UNDERLYING ASSUMPTIONS OF AN INTERPRETIVE APPROACH: THE IMPORTANCE OF LOCAL KNOWLEDGE

What is policy analysis? What does a policy analyst do? Where is she employed?

Common answers to these questions would be that a policy analyst researches a policy issue to advise a policymaker on some decision relative to that issue. The policy analyst provides to the policymaker information that the latter lacks and is unable, for various reasons, to obtain personally. This information has traditionally been some form of technical or other expert knowledge required to craft a policy or to assess the likelihood of and evaluate its projected outcomes, but it may also entail procedural knowledge useful for implementation activities.[1]

Policy analysis has traditionally been undertaken in advance of legislative or other policy-making decisions or acts, but the sphere of activity has also extended to evaluating policies after they have been enacted, and to the evaluation of implementation activities themselves. So Fischer (1995, p. 2), for example, treats policy evaluation as the applied social scientific activity "typically referred to as 'policy analysis' or 'policy science.'" In this view, policy analysis is "designed to supply information about complex social and economic problems and to assess the processes by which a policy or program is formulated and implemented." It can focus on a policy's anticipated outcomes or, in retrospect, on its actual results. Ideally, as Fischer notes, we expect policy analysis to provide both policymakers and citizens "with an intelligent basis for discussing and judging conflicting ideas, proposals, and outcomes."[2]

Professional training in these applied social scientific analytic modes typically takes place in graduate programs in public policy, public administration, planning (urban, city, and regional), social work, education, and other issue-focused departments or schools (such as environmental studies). Even more broadly, as Heineman, Bluhm, Peterson, and Kearny (1990, p. 5) note, physicians, attorneys, and chemists could be said to engage in policy analysis when their work shapes policy decisions. Business and management schools have long taught "business policy" as a central aspect of their curriculum. Even in its current incarnation as business "strategy," this decision-making process follows the same steps as the policy process, even using the same terms (formulation and implementation; see Hatch, 1997, pp. 105-110). Traditional strategic analysis in the business world draws on many of the same tools as traditional policy analysis in assessing and shaping policies with respect to individual and organizational stakeholders, and these traditional approaches face many of the same limitations.

Although policy research can be university-based, it is also supported or conducted by and within independent agencies and consulting firms across the political and topical spectrum (e.g., the Rand Corporation, which also has its own training program; the American Enterprise Institute; the Brookings Institution; and Abt Associates), as well as by legislative aides for state and federal representatives and committees, and by interest groups (e.g., Sierra Club; Peace Officers Research Association of California). Private sector businesses and corporations have increasingly been employing policy analysts to monitor governmental regulations that may affect their activities.

The analytic reports of working policy analysts typically circulate in-house (within whatever agency, community group, or governmental entity commissioned the study, and perhaps among policy-relevant stakeholders). In a revised form, reports may find wider audiences through research papers presented at conferences of such professional associations as APPAM (the Association for Public Policy Analysis and Management), IPSA or APSA (International Political Science Association, American Political Science Association) and regional affiliates (especially in their public policy and public administration sections), and ASPA (American Society for Public Administration), and through more conceptual, theoretical treatments published in such journals as *JPAM* (*Journal of Policy Analysis and Management*), the *Policy Studies Review*, *Policy Studies Journal*, and *Policy Sciences* (not to mention conferences and journals devoted to specific policy areas). Policy analyses are also written initially (and sometimes exclusively) in an academic mode, for conference presentation and journal publication. Whereas the intended reader of "in-house" reports is the policymaker (including implementors), the intended reader of the academic paper is the research community.[3]

In short, policy analysis is conducted at federal, state, regional, and local levels of government; in private, public, and nonprofit realms; by liberals and conservatives; and by single interest groups and those that cover a broader spectrum. This text is written with the understanding that policy analysts work in many capacities:

- as advisers to policymakers;
- as advocates for community groups or as community organizers;
- as staff in nonprofit agencies or lobbying groups.

The text is also written with the understanding that policy analysis is a form of research, and so it speaks to those training or involved in the academic pursuit of policy research as well as to those training or involved in the practices of policy analysis.

Both analytic acts and the spheres of activity, however, have been conceptually curtailed and directed by the research and analytic methods available in training programs and acceptable to policy analysis scholars. If, for example, cost-benefit analysis is accepted as the tool, that is what policy analysts are trained to do. By "accepted" I mean that a method is the basis of papers delivered at associational meetings and published in mainstream journals, thereby developing expectations for professional training and hence becoming the subject of textbooks and the focus of graduate school and other training curricula.[4]

Authors of two recently published textbooks, for example, list a policy analytic process of eight steps and six steps, respectively, one that is fairly commonly identified. The first steps of both are: establish the context, formulate/define the problem, specify objectives/determine evaluation criteria, and explore/evaluate alternatives (Bonser, McGregor, & Oster, 1996;

Patton & Sawicki, 1993). This appears to suggest that the policy analyst generates issue knowledge in a void, from his head. Nowhere does it ask which or whose policy knowledge should be included in these steps or how to access such knowledge.

If, however, we could get out of this cycle of expectations and back to the kinds of acts (including decisions) that the policy process actually entails, we would see that policy actions are not restricted to the sorts of questions amenable to cost-benefit analysis, decision analysis, and so on. There is a realm of activity that policymakers need to have evaluated, systematically, rigorously, and methodically, which centers not only on values but also on other forms of human meaning, including beliefs and feelings. Rebuilding bridges to make them earthquake-ready, or adopting welfare programs, entails judgments about what people *in the situation* find meaningful. For example, a recent health policy survey sought to explore attitudes across American race-ethnic groups about sending infirm elderly parents to nursing homes. The question was meaningless, however, to those who take it as a given that parents will be cared for at home until death: they had no conceptual framework within which to understand the question, which had been generated from the context of a different meaning system of values, beliefs, and feelings. In another example, an American-initiated comparative study of U.S. and Japanese policies included the seemingly innocuous, factual question, "What is your age?" Because of American sensitivities about age, the question was placed at the end of the questionnaire, allowing the researcher and the informant time to establish some rapport that would "cushion" the impact of the question's "personal" nature. When administered in Japan, however, this placement cost researchers key information relative to the elderly informants' status (age being more venerated in Japan than in the United States, broadly speaking), which led to mis-cues in the appropriate phrasing of preceding questions. Moreover, the comparative reliability of these data could be challenged: because of the link between age and status, Japanese answers are more likely to be chronologically accurate (the elderly having no reason to make themselves appear older), whereas Americans are more likely not to respond or to bias their answers toward lower numbers, given the societal value placed on youth.[5] In both cases, survey research missed what was meaningful to policy-relevant publics.

Policy analyses that seek to avoid these sorts of errors and pitfalls require another set of analytic tools, ones based on philosophical presuppositions that put human meaning and social realities at their heart. To understand the consequences of a policy for the broad range of people it will affect requires "local knowledge"—the very mundane, expert understanding of and practical reasoning about local conditions derived from lived experience.[6] Had researchers in either of these examples first sought to understand the values, beliefs, and feelings of informants (about parental aging, about age), and then used that local knowledge in designing the surveys, these problems would likely have been avoided.

The lack of attention to (at best) or outright devaluing of (at worst) local knowledge has been common in development policies. In the 1970s, for example, policies to remedy drought in a specific region had nomadic tribespeople dig more wells. Policy analysts did not understand that, because of the meaning of livestock to a tribesman's reputation, adding wells would encourage him to increase his herd size, thereby leading to an exacerbation of the problem the policy was intended to resolve.[7] Examples from other policy areas abound. Schmidt (1993) writes of the disastrous collapse of a bridge after site-based engineers' "intimate knowledge" about cement requirements under local conditions was dismissed by policymakers in Washington. In connection with nuclear fallout from Chernobyl and sheep grazing in northern England, Wynne (1992) describes the local, implicit knowledge held by shepherds, which was ignored by experts advising policymakers, with detrimental economic results. Had policymakers understood what busing meant to white parents, they might have pursued differently the policy that led to "white flight," which undermined the policy's purpose (Paris & Reynolds, 1983, pp. 180-181).[8] To acquire such local knowledge, policy analysts need interpretive methods.

Interpretive Presuppositions

Interpretive methods are based on the presupposition that we live in a social world characterized by the possibilities of multiple interpretations. In this world there are no "brute data" whose meaning is beyond dispute. Dispassionate, rigorous science is possible—but not the neutral, objective science stipulated by traditional analytic methods (as represented by the scientific method). As living requires sensemaking, and sensemaking entails interpretation, so too does policy analysis.[9]

Traditional approaches to policy analysis—using the tools of microeconomics, decision analysis, and others—are conducted under the assumptions of positivist-informed science: that it is not only necessary but also actually possible, to make objective, value-free assessments of a policy from a point external to it. When policy language is examined, for example, a comparison is often made between the words of legislation and the projected or implemented actions in the field, under the assumption that policy words can and should have univocal, unambiguous meanings that can and should be channeled to and directly apperceived by implementors and policy-relevant publics. These are not the assumptions of this book. This text assumes, rather, that it is not possible for an analyst to stand outside of the policy issue being studied, free of its values and meanings and of the analyst's own values, beliefs, and feelings. The argument assumes that knowledge is acquired through interpretation, which necessarily is "subjective": it reflects the education, experience, and training, as well as the individual, familial, and communal background, of the "subject" making the analysis. Not only analysts, but all actors in a policy situation (as with other aspects of the social world), interpret issue data as they seek to make sense of the policy. Furthermore, human artifacts and actions, including policy documents, legislation, and implementation, are understood here to be not only instrumentally rational but also expressive—of meaning(s), including at times individual and collective identity.[10]

The conceptual bases for these ideas were developed by the mostly German neo-Kantian (or neo-idealist) philosophers in the late 19th century, the phenomenologists and hermeneutic scholars of the early part of the 20th century, and some of the critical theorists of the mid- and late-20th century. They were largely arguing against, first, the insistence of the late-19th-century empirio-criticists that scientific knowledge about the human, social world could be derived only through the five senses—an approach that separates values from facts, leaves values outside of the realm of scientific analysis, and takes no account of Kant's assertion regarding the role of a priori knowledge in understanding. Second, they argued against the early-20th-century logical positivists' and analytical philosophers' reduction (as the critics saw it) of analytic concern to language and its forms of logic. In brief, phenomenologists understood that something—variously called "mind," "consciousness," a *weltanschauung*, "paradigm," "frame," or "lens"—"filters" sense perceptions and organizes perceived physical stimuli (light or sound waves, sensations of taste, touch, smell) in a process of sensemaking. Prior knowledge —whether derived from education, training, experience, or some other form of personal background—was understood to play a central role in sensemaking. Hermeneuticists argued that human meaning was projected into the full range of human artifacts (language, music, art, literature, architecture, acts and interactions, physical objects, and so on) by their creators, and that these artifacts could be studied to gain knowledge of those meanings using the same analytic methods that

had been developed to understand biblical texts (the original arena of hermeneutic analysis).[11]
These ideas became increasingly known in the United States when many of their proponents arrived as refugees from the Nazis. Here, their ideas intersected at times with the work of John Dewey and George Herbert Mead, contributing to the development of symbolic interactionism and ethnomethodology.[12] These ideas began to enter the realm of the policy sciences in the 1970s and 1980s, through the work of Murray Edelman, Martin Rein and Donald Schon, John Dryzek, Frank Fischer, Bruce Jennings, David Paris and James Reynolds, Douglas Torgerson, Mary Hawkesworth, and Deborah Stone.[13] Articles published in the pages of the journal *Policy Sciences* during the 1980s and first part of the 1990s were also influential[14]—although, as Torgerson (1985) notes, some of these ideas can be traced to the work of Harold Lasswell. (Certainly, Lasswell and his colleagues were interested in the communication of meaning, although they took their content analysis in a different methodological direction than that used by contemporary interpretive analysts; see Lasswell, Leites, & Associates, 1949; Lasswell, Lerner, & De Sola Pool, 1952.)

This conceptual work was bolstered by parallel developments in the areas of program evaluation and policy implementation, particularly through the work of Egon Guba and Yvonna Lincoln (1989) and several of the essays in the works of Palumbo and Calista (1987, 1990).[15] At the same time, many policy analytic theorists were influenced by interpretive work from other fields, in particular developments in symbolic anthropology, especially the work of Clifford Geertz (1973, 1983); in the philosophy and history of science, including the arguments of Kuhn (1962), Latour (1987), and Rorty (1979); in literary theory (e.g., Fish, 1980); and in contemporary political philosophy (e.g., Habermas, 1987; Ricoeur, 1971; Taylor, 1971; and others).[16]

By and large, the work to date in interpretive policy analysis has focused on its underlying philosophical positions. Much of it has taken the shape of an argument against the positivist philosophical presuppositions underlying traditional policy analytic approaches, concerning the reality of the social world and our ability to know and understand it. In the traditional view, science and social science are seen as mirroring nature and the social world, rather than as constituting human interpretations of those worlds.[17] The interpretive approach is less an argument (in the context of policy analysis, at least) contesting the nature of reality than one about the human possibilities of knowing the world around us and the character of that knowledge.

Interpretive approaches to policy analysis focus on the meanings that policies have for a broad range of policy-relevant publics, including but not limited to clients and potential clients, legislators, cognate agencies (supportive and contesting), implementors (such as implementing-agency executives, administrators, and staff), and potential voters. Luker (1984), for example, argues that debates about abortion policy are less disagreements about facts than they are contests over the threatened loss of public sanctioning of a set of values, beliefs, and feelings. Her analysis focuses on women arguing and enacting these positions, rather than on policymakers or agency personnel. Interpretive approaches, like hers, explore not only "what" specific policies mean but also "how" they mean—through what processes policy meanings are communicated and who their intended audiences are, as well as what context-specific meanings these and other "readers" make of policy artifacts. In doing so, they consider the acts of legislators and decision makers, and the actions of implementing agencies, to be potentially as central in communicating policy meanings as the enabling legislation itself. In including agency actions, policy analysis draws on ideas from organizational studies (including that aspect of public administration) as much as it does on ideas about policy processes developed within political science.

Interpretive analyses often focus on "puzzles" or "tensions" of two related sorts. The first is the difference between what the analyst expects to find and what she actually experiences in the policy or agency field. The expectations that one brings to a policy analytic project derive from one's prior experience, education, or training. When there is a "mismatch," the ensuing puzzle or tension creates the opportunity to explain why the policy or agency is doing things "differently." The impulse, often, is to assume that the different way is "wrong": "They" don't know how to do things "right." An interpretive approach urges us to treat such differences as different ways of seeing, understanding, and doing, based on different prior experiences. This does not mean that all positions are necessarily "right," but it does call on the analyst (if not contending parties) to accord different views and their underlying feelings serious respect. They are not likely to be changed by appeal to facts alone (and coercive change is not an option). If we can uncouple "different" from "wrong," we can, in this view, proceed in another fashion.[18] In analytic projects, the tension between expectations and present experience is a potential source of insight, and should be dwelled on, even cherished, although many analysts might be tempted to resolve the tension immediately. That tension is produced by the juxtaposition of the analyst's "estrangement" from the analytic situation and her growing familiarity with that situation. By prolonging the balance between "stranger-ness" and "insider-ness," the analyst is able to move back and forth between seeing things as they are and seeing them as they are not.

A commonplace example might be school board hearings, in which parents argue based on their remembered experiences as students, whereas teachers and principals argue based on more recent developments in, for example, learning theory. In land use planning issues, city planners have visions of things as they should be based on good design principles, whereas residents foresee a host of problems ensuing from living with the plan's implementation. In both cases, a policy analyst would be far more productive in helping the parties understand the differences underlying one another's positions—that they are situated knowers arguing from different standpoints (rather than attributing stupidity or "blindness" to reality to the opposing side)—than by providing econometric data.

The second sort of puzzlement that can spark interpretive analysis derives from the tension captured in the admonition to "Do as I say, not as I do," invoked so often by parents speaking to their children. Children (and sometimes workplace subordinates) are admonished in this way in the face of the very anticipation that they will do precisely what they see their parents (or superiors) do, rather than following what they are told to do. And, indeed, psychological research (e.g., Rosenhan, Frederick, & Burrowes, 1968) bears this out: when faced with a contradiction between word and deed, we tend to believe that the deed is closer to the truth (or to the individual's intentions) than the word.

In policy terms, this translates into believing that what implementors do, rather than what the policy "says" in its explicit language, constitutes the "truth" of policy (and thereby the state's) intent. This is one of the points that Lipsky (1979) and his colleagues (Prottas, 1979; Weatherley, 1979) made in analyzing street-level bureaucrats, their agencies, and their clients. Policy analysis, in this view, cannot be restricted to policy language or ideas only as understood and intended by their authors. Others whose understandings of the policy are or will be central to its enactment are also of analytic concern. Interpretive policy analysis explores the contrasts between policy meanings as intended by policymakers —"authored" texts—and the possibly variant and even incommensurable meanings —"constructed" texts— made of them by other policy-relevant groups. Much of policy analysis, especially ex post implementation or evaluation analysis, requires the establishment of policy intent as a benchmark against which to assess enactments or outcomes. This is the sense of the policy as established by its creators—the authored text. But what interpretive analysis leads us to see is that it would be erroneous to assume that this is the only meaning appropriate or relevant for assessment. As implementation problems are often created by different understandings of policy language, it is as important for analysts to access these other interpretations—the local knowledge held by communities of meaning in constructed texts.[19]

Communities of Meaning and Policy Frames: The Architecture of Policy Arguments

Through a process of interaction, members of a community—whether a community of scientists or environmentalists or some other group—come to use the same or similar cognitive mechanisms, engage in the same or similar acts, and use the same or similar language to talk about thought and action. Group processes reinforce these, often promoting internal cohesion as an identity marker with respect to other communities: the familiar "us-them" phenomenon. Although the language of "community" has its roots in a geographic locale—connoting similarities of position deriving from shared property-based interests, political views, race-ethnicity, class, religion, or other commonalities—it is borrowed into a policy context with broader reference points, which are not place-specific: "location" within an organizational structure, professional training and membership, sex and gender, and myriad other possible dimensions lead to a set of values, beliefs, and feelings that can bind people together in communities of meaning.[20] Cognitive, linguistic, and cultural practices reinforce each other, to the point at which shared sense is more common than not, and policy-relevant groups become "interpretive communities" sharing thought, speech, practice, and their meanings.[21] Such communities may be fluid, changing from issue to issue (although often with some overlap, e.g., according to positions along a spectrum of political or religious ideology). In Chapter 2 we shall explore how to identify these communities.

The preceding discussion suggests the existence of at least three communities of meaning in any policy situation: policymakers, implementing agency personnel, and affected citizens or clients. But we know from implementation and organizational studies that agencies may contain any number of internal communities of meaning: directors, managers or administrators, groups of professionals, lower-level employees, and street-level bureaucrats.[22] And from community studies we know that communities and neighborhoods have internal divisions. We also know that the issues of policy debate do not die once a piece of legislation has been passed: they survive and resurface in subsequent debates, as well as in implementation actions

(Baier, March, & Saetren, 1986; Yanow, 1993). Moreover, there are many other policy-relevant groups—community residents, cognate and competing agencies and professionals, interest groups, potential clients, unheard or silent voices; which ones are of analytic and decision-making concern will depend on the specific policy issue in question—each one of which may interpret the policy differently from legislators' intent (if that can even be established as a single meaning). Rather than assuming, then, that policy problems are objectively "factual" in character and searching for the single correct formulation of a policy statement, policy analysts might take the alternative view that problem statements are contending interpretations of policy issues made by different communities of meaning.[23] This is what Luker (1984) did in analyzing abortion policy debates.

The central question, then, for interpretive policy analysts is, How is the policy issue being framed by the various parties to the debate? A "frame"— with its metaphoric origins in a picture frame, the photographer's framing of a scene through the viewfinder, the skeletal frame of a house under construction—sets up an interpretive framework within which policy-related artifacts make sense. Whether a hand gesture is seen as a wave or as a cry for help—the driving force of Stevie Smith's poem "Not waving but drowning" (Smith, 1972)—depends on how it is framed. Frames direct attention toward some elements while simultaneously diverting attention from other elements. They highlight and contain at the same time that they exclude. That which is highlighted or included is often that which the framing group values. Frame conflict occurs not only because different interpretive communities focus cognitively and rationally on different elements of a policy issue, but because they value different elements differently. The different frames reflect groups' values contending for public recognition and validation.[24]

Joseph Gusfield's analysis of Temperance, Prohibition, and Repeal (1963) provides an extended example. Prohibitionists, largely native-born, rural, Protestant, and middle class, finding their values under attack from the increasing numbers and public presence of immigrant, urban, Catholic lower classes, used legislative politics to attempt to quiet "the fear that their own abstainer's culture was not really the criterion by which respectability was judged in the dominant areas of the total society" (p. 110). Ratification of the Prohibition amendment was understood as a public affirmation of "dry" norms. The vote for Prohibition represented symbolically the power, prestige, and hence dominance of those norms and the people who practiced them, despite the difficulties of its enforcement. While opponents framed Prohibition as, among other things, an attack on individual liberties, proponents argued for it in an expression of status and identity. Prohibitionists used legislation to make a public identity statement, to themselves as well as to their opposition, that validated one set of meanings—of values, beliefs, and feelings—over another.

Frames are often expressed through language. There is a complex interrelationship among language, cognition (or perception), and action. It is not entirely clear which one shapes (or causes) the other: do we understand (or see) housing as decaying because the concept is available to us, or do we develop the language of decay because we understand housing to be falling apart? Or does that understanding come about because we observe and know our bodies to decay?[25] That debate, long-standing in cognitive linguistics, perceptual psychology, and philosophy, will not be resolved here, but it is important for our discussion. Policy frames use language, especially metaphoric language, and in so doing shape perceptions and understandings. Housing policy in the United States during the 1960s and 1970s, for example, encapsulated in the phrase "urban renewal," was framed as protecting residents from housing "decay." The notion of "decay" has its metaphoric source in natural settings—wood decays, teeth decay—and housing policy language drew on common understanding of those metaphoric origins.

Importantly, frames also entail courses of action. We know how we would proceed in the case of tooth decay: We would consult a dentist, a specialist in that field, for treatment. In the case of housing decay, then, we proceed accordingly and consult a "housing doctor," a specialist in urban renewal.[26] Or, in another example from the 1960s and 1970s, "broken homes" were treated in welfare policy in a fashion analogous to broken china: policies were designed to patch them up, to glue the pieces back together. In this instance, there was no frame conflict at that time (although today we treat the same family configuration as "single parent families," a frame that contains no sense of a need for governmental reparative intervention). In the case of housing policy, however, a contending view did emerge shortly after many neighborhoods were bulldozed. "Urban renewal" was seen as rending the "social fabric" that had been "woven" by neighborhood residents and that "bound" them together. Indeed, at least one study tracked the psychological dislocation felt by "slum" residents who were relocated to new public housing (Fried, 1963). Contending frames entail not just different policy discourses—different language, understandings, and perceptions—and potentially different courses of action, but also different values, and different meanings.[27] The role of the interpretive policy analyst is to map the "architecture" of debate relative to the policy issue under investigation, by identifying the language and its entailments (understandings, actions, meanings) used by different interpretive communities in their framing of the issue.[28] For example, in his analysis of the electromagnetic frequency (EMF) cancer controversy, Stephen Linder (1995) identified five communities of meaning with their attendant discourses and expectations of policy intervention (what he calls "construction[s] of a public remedy," p. 213). At the time of his analysis, scientific evidence to support the causal linkage was inconclusive. The five interpretive communities framed the EMF problem as:

- a "public health emergency" (argued by critics of the electric power industry);
- a "threat to the public's welfare" (the argument of state authorities, such as public utility commissions [PUCs]);
- a shortage of sufficient information, leading to "growing public apprehension" (an argument appealing to individual responsibility and choice);
- "the spread of premature . . . controls" (argued by some within the electric power industry);
- prematurely heightened concern based on "inconclusive scientific research" (argued by others within the electric power industry). (pp. 218-224)

Linder identified these five thought-speech-interpretive communities and their respective stances by analyzing the language used by PUCs, state health departments, citizens' groups, and others as it appeared in agency reports, hearings testimony, reportage, opinion pieces, and so on. Each frame entailed not only a construction of the EMF issue but also anticipation of appropriate governmental action. To map the architecture of the EMF debate he needed to access this intimate, local knowledge of their own situations and what was meaningful to them.

Whether we treat "frame" as a noun or as a verb also has implications for the form of our analytic study.[29] "Frame" as a noun suggests a comparative analysis across communities of meaning, at a (relatively) fixed point in time, of the various ways in which a policy issue has been "framed," that is, interpreted and understood. "Frame" as a verb suggests a more dynamic analysis of changes in issue "framing" over time, possibly within a single community of meaning. These two types of study suggest different constituencies: the duration and depth of the latter suggest perhaps a more academic interest in understanding interpretive processes; the former suggests more of an issue focus, whether for academic or policy-making purposes (or both).

Symbolic Relationships
and Tacit Knowledge

An interpretive approach to policy analysis, then, is one that focuses on the meanings of policies, on the values, feelings, or beliefs they express, and on the processes by which those meanings are communicated to and "read" by various audiences. How might a researcher-analyst identify these meanings? Interpretive philosophies, such as phenomenology and hermeneutics, contend that human meanings, values, beliefs, and feelings are embodied in and transmitted through artifacts of human creation, such as language, dress, patterns of action and interaction, written texts, or built spaces. In the context of policy analysis, this means focusing on policy or agency artifacts as the concrete symbols representing more abstract policy and organizational meanings.

A symbol is something—usually concrete—that represents something else—usually an abstraction. For example, a dove is a symbol of peace.[30] A symbol is a social convention: a group of people (a state, a society, a tribe, an organization, a community, a workgroup) agree on it as a stand-in for the meaning(s) it conveys. Policy, agency, and community analysis treat public, not private or personal, symbols and their meanings. And these are historically and culturally specific: at another time, in another place, for another group of people, a dove could be dinner or simply a grayish white bird.

Symbols serve to unite those who share their meanings, while setting them apart from other people or groups who do not. Knowing these names, traditions, and other symbols is itself important as a symbol of membership in the nation, community, organization, or group. "Not to know them is not to belong" (Hunter, 1974, p. 67).

Because of this context specificity, a symbol may accommodate several meanings. The home provided by housing policy may represent security, status, shelter, and wealth. Different individuals, reflecting the different groups of which they are members, may interpret the same symbol differently. In the EMF example, Linder (1995) discovered that the artifact that held different meaning for different people was the EMF power lines themselves, as expressed in the language used to talk about them: they represented, symbolically, the presence of technology in a residential area and a range of attitudes toward the meaning of "science" (and technology). The power of symbols lies in their potential to accommodate multiple meanings.[31]

Human artifacts stand in a symbolic (that is, representational) relationship to the meaning(s) they embody or engender. The symbols embody

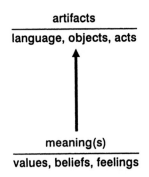

Figure 1.1 Meanings (values, beliefs, feelings) are embedded in policy artifacts (language, objects, acts) in a symbolic (representational) relationship.

three dimensions of human meaning-making: emotive/aesthetic (pathos), cognitive (logos), and moral (ethos), corresponding to feelings, values, and beliefs (Gagliardi, 1990). They come to be more visible and tangible evidence of the values, beliefs, and feelings that a group holds, believes in, and practices. Artifactual symbols include three broad categories of human action: language, objects, and acts. As shown in Figure 1.1, the artifact is the concrete manifestation or expression of the more abstract value, belief, feeling, or meaning.

The process of creating, sustaining, and changing artifacts and their meanings is a dynamic one, and so a second arrow needs to be added to the figure, moving from artifact to meaning. Each time we engage, invoke, or use an artifact, we reinforce, maintain, or change its underlying meaning(s) (Figure 1.2).

Meanings, being abstract, are difficult to know about or discover directly. They are hard to "pin down," to make concrete and imageable. In part, this is because values and meanings are often known tacitly, rather than explicitly. We typically do not speak to one another about our values and beliefs in everyday encounters in the post office or on the street (e.g., "Hello, I'm John and I value freedom and individuality"); or if we do, we often present what we think we believe or value, or think we ought to value, or what we would like the other person to perceive as our value, yet these may not be the values we act out. For example, Mary, observing John, may ask him to corroborate or correct her interpretation. But asking John to state his values absent an action context may elicit a story about the values he preaches rather than those he practices, and the two are often different.[32]

16

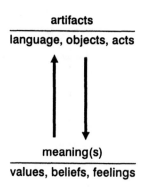

Figure 1.2 The use of artifacts maintains or changes their underlying meanings.

Nevertheless, we do know a great deal about what others value and believe: although not spoken of directly, others' values, beliefs, and feelings are tacitly known, and communicated through the artifacts that express them—the objects, language, and acts of everyday life. These have acquired meaning in certain contexts, and members of those contexts share those meanings. We know—because we have learned through socialization and other forms of teaching—how to interpret the meanings of artifactual symbols in their contexts. We communicate, in other words, through "artifactual interaction," our often daily engagement with symbolic language, objects, and acts, interpreting the more concrete symbolic representations (for example, John's clothes, posture, gestures, reported observations, and the like) that embody our and others' values, beliefs, feelings, and meanings. We are able to understand one another without always making meanings explicit, by drawing on tacit knowledge of the symbols' meanings. This is especially true of nonverbal language (posture, dress, gestures, and so on) and built space and its "props" (e.g., landscaping, furnishings, decor).[33] As Polanyi (1966, p. 4) noted with regard to tacit knowledge, we "know much more than we can tell." The consequence of Mary's holding a certain value or belief or feeling in a particular way may be understood by observing her actions and interpreting them, inferring from action to meaning(s). By interpreting such symbols, we strive to understand the meanings they are vested with and their moral (belief), cognitive (value), and affective (feeling) bases. Our understanding may be wrong—we have made an interpretation that is not in keeping with the actor's intent; but in acting on that interpretation, we may discover our error.

All language, objects, and acts are potential carriers of meaning, open to interpretation by legislators, implementors, clients or policy "targets," concerned publics, and other stakeholders. At the same time, in their use, they are tools for the re-creation of those meanings and for the creation of new meanings. Through artifactual interaction, we re-embody them with meaning at the same time that we use them to communicate those meanings and to create extensions of those meanings. It is important to emphasize the contextual nature of such knowledge. Although symbolic meanings need not necessarily be "local" meanings in a geographic sense, they are "local" in a policy issue sense. It is also important to note that it is only provisional knowledge, subject to change as circumstances and individuals change or as our (mis)interpretations are corrected.[34] This lack of universality and eternity stands in marked contrast to positivist notions of the certainty of knowledge.

This focus on interpretation of meanings made by actors in policy and agency contexts lies at the heart of an interpretive ontological, epistemological, and methodological stance. In this sense, the methods of interpretive analysis that focus on the ways in which meanings are made and conveyed are, at the same time, the subjects of study. The medium of communication is intimately connected with the message it communicates.[35]

Texts, "Text Analogues," and Interpretive Communities

We complicate the picture further if we consider not only public policies as texts that are interpreted as they are enacted by implementors, but also those enactments themselves as "texts" that are "read" by various stakeholder groups: clients, potential clients, legislators, other agency personnel, other citizens, and, at times, "foreigners" as well. It is helpful here to borrow some concepts from literary theory and criticism, which have long been concerned with how texts convey meaning. Reader-response theory—a literary theory of textual meaning developed since the 1970s—refutes earlier theories that the meaning of a text derives from the text alone (its language, form, or both) or from its author's intentions. Rather, a text's meaning derives also from what the reader brings to it (see, e.g., Iser, 1989). In one view, meaning resides not in any one of these—not exclusively in the author's intent, in the text itself, or in the reader alone—but is, rather, created actively in interactions among all three, in the writing and in the reading.

In this sense, not only is legislative and other language a text that is interpreted by implementors and others, but those interpretations—in the form of implementing agency language, objects, and acts—themselves become "texts" that are "read" by those actors and others. A text or "text-analogue" (Taylor, 1971; see also Ricoeur, 1971)—that is, act, object, or spoken language treated as text—is interpreted by its "readers"—agency staff, clients, and so forth. But these interpretations prompt or come in the form of responses—acts, language, or objects—which themselves are then treated as texts and interpreted.[36]

Reader-response theory underscores the methodological approach outlined here for exploring where meaning resides, directing the researcher-analyst not to policy language or legislators' intent alone, but to "readers'" interpretations as well. This means that interpretive analysts no longer see or treat clients (for example) as passive "targets" of policy "missiles" (the military metaphor underlying traditional policy analysis), but as active constructors of meaning as they "read" legislative language and agency objects and acts.[37] Implementation difficulties, in this view, may no longer be fixed by repairing ambiguous policy language, because in this view not only is language inherently multivocal—capable of carrying multiple meanings—but clients' and others' interpretations cannot be predetermined or controlled.

Two additional levels of textual interpretation need to be mentioned here, although I will not develop this idea until Chapter 6. First, in producing a report, the analyst is himself engaged in interpretive acts. Whether reporting on observations, on interviews, or on documents, the analyst presents his interpretation of what he has seen, done, heard, and/or read. Second, the reader of this report also interprets. And so we have not only the immediacy of first-level interpretations (made by actors in the situation) and the less proximate characteristic of second-level interpretations (made by the nonparticipating researcher-analyst), but the reader's even more distant third level, as illustrated in Figure 1.3.[38]

What this underscores is that policy analysis cannot be conducted from a position external to what is being studied. Although interpretive analysis uses systematic, rigorous methods, these methods do not lead to universal, objective claims. Much as Heisenberg argued in the context of physics that the presence of an observer affects the actions of the observed, here, too, one cannot escape interpreting.[39]

This implies a different role for policy analysts from the traditional production of numerical analyses of policy "facts": clarifying the varying interpretations of policy meanings made by different groups, as well as understanding the various elements through which these meanings are communicated. Some interpretive analysts would also add a third role: ensuring that underrepresented groups are enabled to make their interpreta-

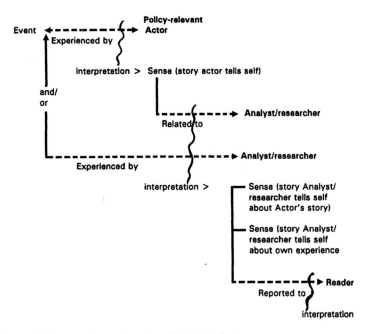

Figure 1.3 Sensemaking and levels of interpretation.

tions heard. This last position argues for interpretive policy analysis as a more democratic mode (see, for example, Schneider and Ingram, 1993, and the essays in Fischer and Forester, 1993) than traditional policy analysis, which rests on the technocratic expertise of its practitioners.[40] This is not the traditional view of a policy process as a legislative (or even institutional) agenda controlled solely by public decision makers determining the course of future policies. Interpretive analysts develop and practice an expertise in the methodical processes of accessing local knowledge and mapping the architecture of policy debates, but they treat policy, agency, and community members—the actors in the situation—as the substantive experts of their own domains. Interpretive policy analysts, in this view, put their skills to the service of many groups, not just elected officials. Out of this conversation among multiple voices, perhaps (and ideally) the interpretive analyst can help generate new ideas for policy action—possibly by synthesizing opposing arguments or reframing the debate at another level (Roe, 1994)—rather than merely advising on the choice of one existing proposal over the others.

Steps to an Interpretive Policy Analysis:
Mapping Issue Architecture

Because of the abstract, less accessible, and less observable nature of meanings, interpretive research proceeds from an identification and analysis of the more concrete, more observable, and more accessible artifacts which embody the more abstract meanings. The first two steps in interpretive policy analysis are to identify the artifacts that are significant carriers of meaning for the interpretive communities relative to a given policy issue, and to identify those communities relevant to the policy issue that create or interpret these artifacts and meanings. Conceptually, either of these can precede the other; each leads to the other. In practice, both are conducted at the same time, weaving back and forth between artifact and interpretive community. Informed by the assumption that we live in a world of multiple possible interpretations, the analyst needs to explore the existence of different interpretations of each artifact (thereby leading to different interpretive communities) or the existence of different interpretive communities (some of which may find meaning in different artifacts).

The third step conceptually, but also conducted in the process of the first two, is to identify the communities' "discourses": how they talk and act with respect to the policy issue. The goal of this step is to be able to say something about the meanings—the values, beliefs, feelings—that are important to each policy-relevant community, as well as to extend the analysis of the artifacts. Since these meanings are largely known tacitly, and are therefore hard to access directly, it is necessary to identify the artifacts—the language, objects, and acts—in which they are embedded, and which represent them in a symbolic fashion (as diagrammed in Figure 1.1).

But since we are speaking of interpretive communities that may find different meanings in the same policy artifacts, this diagram needs modification, as shown in Figure 1.4.

The third step, then, is to identify the various meanings carried by specific artifacts for those different interpretive communities. In the fourth step the analyst identifies the meanings that are in conflict between or among groups and their conceptual sources.

Although a researcher might stop at this point, this is where intervention begins. What that intervention might look like will depend on the specific context of analysis, including the particular policy and the role of the analyst. A policy analyst advising a policymaker might take the next step of showing the policymaker the implications of the different and conflicting meanings for the implementation of the proposed policy. Is implementation

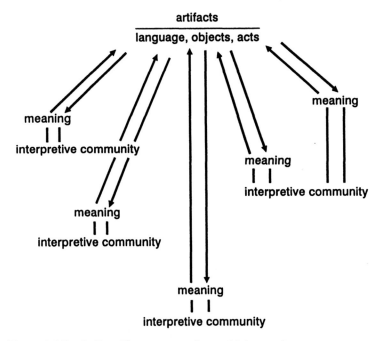

Figure 1.4 Symbolic artifacts accommodate multiple meanings.

likely to founder because one or another group will not "buy in" to the proposed program, because of what that program means to that group? A policy analyst advising community groups or agencies might show that the differences of opinion between them and other groups or agencies derive from different experiences, backgrounds, and so forth, and that these represent different ways of seeing rather than groundless obstinacy or any of the other myriad ways people have of dismissing opposing views. Pal (1995), for example, shows how policy analysts can play a role in helping members of contending interpretive communities "understand that they have epistemological and ethical differences, not merely differences over priorities" (p. 202), which shape as well as derive from their access to and treatment of local knowledge.[41]

The last step analytic practice might take could be in the form of negotiation or mediation, in which conflicting interpretations would be identified and explained as such. It is an educative process that takes as its goal the fostering of discussion honoring the reality of entrenched viewpoints,

Table 1.1. Steps in Interpretive Policy Analysis

1. Identify the artifacts (language, objects, acts) that are significant carriers of meaning for a given policy issue, as perceived by policy-relevant actors and interpretive communities

2. Identify communities of meaning/interpretation/speech/practice that are relevant to the policy issue under analysis

3. Identify the "discourses": the specific meanings being communicated through specific artifacts and their entailments (in thought, speech, and act)

4. Identify the points of conflict and their conceptual sources (affective, cognitive, and/or moral) that reflect different interpretations by different communities

Interventions/Actions

5a. Show implications of different meanings/interpretations for policy formulation and/or action

5b. Show that differences reflect different ways of seeing

5c. Negotiate/mediate/intervene in some other form to bridge differences (e.g., suggest reformulation or reframing)

Note: Steps 1 and 2 lead to each other; 1, 2, and 3 are typically done at the same time.

while nonetheless seeking engaged discourse and debate among policy-relevant publics. The role of the analyst may be to guide the policymaker's choice of one of the existing options. But she may also play a role in enabling the reframing of those options or the policy question itself, thereby leading to a new understanding among contesting parties that points to new avenues for action.[42]

These steps are summarized in Table 1.1.

The distinctions among these steps are conceptual. In practice they are often intertwined: analysis proceeds by tacking back and forth among them.

Similarly, while I treat the three broad categories of artifacts—language, objects, and acts—as distinct analytic lenses, in practice there is overlap among them: each often entails the use of the others. Each category allows an analytic focus that shifts or disappears when looking through another lens, however; so for the sake of analytical clarity I will treat them separately to organize the data analysis methods presented in Chapters 3 through 5.

Summary

Interpretive policy analysis:

1. emphasizes, in methodology as well as other philosophical concerns, the meaningfulness of human action;

2. seeks to understand the intentions underlying actors' practical reasoning[43] in particular situations: What are *their* conceptual boxes (not the analyst's or the decision maker's alone)? How did *they* make sense of the situation?

3. treats artifacts conceptually as texts, as a way of understanding their meaning to their creators ("authors") as well as to other policy-relevant publics ("readers"), thereby explaining how a policy event or artifact makes sense in a particular context—the context of the culture (the set of meanings and their artifactual embodiments) that comprises the agency or organization (or part of one), the community, and/or the polity or society (at the local, regional, state, or national level) in which the policy being analyzed is (to be) enacted;

4. explains the practical reasoning (that is, the intentions underlying the actions) of the actors who engaged the event or artifact.

NOTES

1. See, e.g., the discussion in Fischer (1990).
2. Fischer (1995, p. 3) notes the semantic confusion in the policy literature concerning the terms "policy analysis," "policy science," and "policy evaluation." I follow his lead here in treating these as synonyms for the practice of social scientific analytic activities applied to the domain of public policies. In this sense, as he notes, evaluation research is but one of the methods used in policy analysis. For a succinct history of the development of policy analysis as a field of study and practice, see Heineman et al. (1990), chap. 1.
3. John Van Maanen has drawn my attention to Hammersley's (1993) argument that the potential influence of the two is different: in-house reports potentially have more direct consequences, whereas academic papers are directed more toward theoretical development and hence are often more historical than contemporary. The matter of the usage and practical impact of policy analyses has been a central issue in the field, and this argument joins other explanations of why analytic reports have often not been taken up by policymakers. See, e.g., Lindblom and Cohen (1979) on this point.
4. Latour (1987) provides an extended description of this process in the context of laboratory science; it holds for a wide variety of academic-based practices.
5. This example is based on a discussion of functional and conceptual equivalence in Peng, Peterson, and Shui (1991, p. 101).
6. "Local knowledge" is also the title of a collection of essays by the anthropologist Clifford Geertz (1983). "Practical reasoning" is a term associated with the Aristotelian notion of *phronesis*; see Hawkesworth (1988, pp. 54-57) and Ruderman (1997) for discussions of this concept and some of its contemporary exponents.

24

7. Thurston Clarke, *The last caravan*, New York: Putnam, 1978; cited in Paris and Reynolds (1983, p. 199, n. 9).

8. See also Chock (1995), Colebatch (1995), Hofmann (1995), Linder (1995), and Pal (1995) for other examples of the importance and use of local knowledge in a policy context.

9. This is not a call, in other words, for more interpretation on the part of policy analysts. As Feldman (1988) has noted, "interpretation is already . . . and . . . necessarily happening" (p. 146). It is, however, a call for recognition of that fact in the academy, in its courses, its textbooks, and its research.

10. For an excellent statement and critique of the assumptions of a policy analysis informed by positivist philosophy, see Hawkesworth (1988). See also Paris and Reynolds (1983), especially chapters 1 and 6, which include a critical view of the shortcomings of one form of interpretive analysis. For a critique grounded less in philosophical underpinnings and more in traditional policy analytic practices, see Stone (1988). For discussions that link the philosophical background to methodological concerns, see Bulmer (1986) and Polkinghorne (1983).

11. For background on these thinkers and their ideas, see, e.g., Berger and Luckmann (1966), Bernstein (1976), Burrell and Morgan (1979), Dallmayr and McCarthy (1977), Fay (1975), Filmer et al. (1972), Polkinghorne (1983), and Rabinow and Sullivan (1979). See also Schutz (1962). For philosophical sources of a post-positivist or interpretive approach to policy analysis, including one based on critical theory, see Ascher (1987), Brunner (1982), Dryzek (1982), Fischer (1980), Hawkesworth (1988), Healy (1986), Jennings (1983, 1987), Maynard-Moody and Stull (1987), Paris and Reynolds (1983, especially chaps. 1 and 6), Torgerson (1986b), and Yanow (1996b, chap. 1).

12. On symbolic interactionism, see Charon (1985). On ethnomethodology, see Garfinkel (1977).

13. See Edelman (1964, 1971, 1977), Rein (1976, 1983a), Schon (1979; Rein and Schon, 1977; Schon and Rein, 1994), Fischer (1980), Dryzek (1982), Jennings (1983, 1987), Paris and Reynolds (1983), Torgerson (1985, 1986a, 1986b), Hawkesworth (1988), and Stone (1988).

14. See, e.g., Ascher (1987), Brunner (1982, 1987), Healy (1986), and Yanow (1993, 1995a).

15. See especially the essays in both Palumbo and Calista volumes by Fox, Linder and Peters, Nakamura, and Yanow, and by Ferman in the 1990 edition.

16. There have been parallel developments in interpretive sociology (among them Gusfield [1963, 1981] and Luker [1984]) and in history (e.g., Davis [1983] and Darnton [1984]). And in economics, McCloskey's work (1985) on rhetoric follows similar paths, as does Bruner's (1990) in psychology. The scope of this intellectual ferment is so broad that I can only point the interested reader to some of the works in these different fields. There are many more that could equally well have been mentioned.

17. The notion of science as a "mirror of nature" comes from Rorty (1979).

18. See Minow (1990) on different ways of treating "difference." See also Roe (1994) on treating entrenched differences seriously and according them respect, and Bernstein (1983) on the question of relativism.

19. I am bypassing here the critical question of whether intent can even be established, as well as the point that policy language often contains elements of prior debates, such that more than one intent may be embedded there. See Baier et al. (1986) and Yanow (1993). This line of reasoning parallels that of "original intent" arguments with respect

to the Constitution and the Founding Fathers, engaged publicly around the nomination of Judge Robert Bork to the Supreme Court. See Teuber (1987).

20. And individuals may, and do, belong to multiple interpretive communities. This approach reflects the two senses of "paradigm" described by Kuhn (1962): it is both a worldview and the community of practitioners sharing and articulating that view. Members acquire it through education and training, experience, and practice of their trade, profession, or craft, as well as from familial, communal, and societal or national backgrounds and personality. This also reflects a phenomenological approach (see, e.g., Berger & Luckmann, 1966, Part II; Schutz, 1962).

21. Incorporating thought and speech and practice perhaps accounts for the duality present in Kuhn's (1962) use of paradigm and in some accounts of the hermeneutic circle: both refer to the worldview articulated by members as well as to the community that articulates that view. See Lave and Wenger (1991) on communities of practice.

22. See Raelin (1986) and Lipsky (1979).

23. See, e.g., Dery (1987) on the facticity of policy "facts."

24. The use of "frame" in such a cognitive sense seems to have originated with Bateson (1955). For applications to a policy context, see Rein and Schon (1977) and Schon and Rein (1994). See also Goffman (1974) for a more general social scientific application.

25. The Sapir-Whorf hypothesis suggests that concepts derive from experience. For example, if we did not have the erect, vertical bodies we do and did not consider our brains to be the driving force that we think they are, we might put the "heads" of our corporations (note the Latin root, *corpus*, meaning "body") other than on the top floor at headquarters (body language again)—as, indeed, people in other cultures, such as Ghana and India, have done. See Lakoff and Johnson (1980) on the relationship between orientation metaphors and bodily experience. Cicourel (1964, pp. 34-38) discusses the methodological implications of Sapir-Whorf.

26. Schon (1979) discusses housing decay as a metaphor of disease and health.

27. See, e.g., Rein (1976, 1983b) on values and policy analysis.

28. Pal (1995, p. 202) also talks about mapping the architecture of policy arguments, as we shall see more extensively in Chapter 2.

29. I am indebted to Ralph Brower for articulating this distinction.

30. The following discussion is taken from Yanow (1996b, chap. 1).

31. Langer (1957) distinguishes between "sign" and "symbol." In her view a sign— e.g., a traffic light, a stop sign—is task- or action-oriented. Both are representative; but a sign is more immediately instrumental (p. 63). Although this precise distinction is not universally accepted across philosophy, semiotics, and anthropology, it does point to something of the conceptual range of symbology.

32. Vickers (1973) and others have noted this sort of discrepancy. Again, the admonition "Do as I say, not as I do" echoes this distinction. Argyris and Schon (1974) refer to it as the difference between one's "espoused" theory (what I say) and one's "theory in use" (what I do).

33. See, e.g., Goffman's (1979) wonderful treatment of the language of advertising in the communication of gender meanings, the work of Hall (1959, 1966) on time and space, and Appleyard (1981) and Lynch (1960, 1972) on the vocabulary of street design.

34. This is one understanding of the process described by the "hermeneutic circle": that we begin with one provisional interpretation and then correct it as we learn more.

35. This, of course, was Marshall McLuhan's notion (1964). Edelman (1995) explores such interconnections in the realm of art and politics.

The stance outlined here is represented in some of the work in organizational culture (e.g., Gagliardi, 1990; Turner, 1990). Schein (1985) presents organizational culture as a layering of artifacts, values, and assumptions (p. 14), without noting their representational relationship and the necessity of artifacts for the communication of culture. Deal and Kennedy (1982), by contrast, appear to emphasize only the artifactual component of organizational culture. My argument here is that artifacts are a necessary but not sufficient component of culture. They are linked as embodiments or symbolic representations to their meanings (values, beliefs, feelings). This is a mutually reinforcing and re-creating relationship, carried out through our daily interaction with the artifacts of our creation. But see Hatch (1993) for a different interpretive approach in the context of organizational culture.

36. The reference in the preceding paragraph to Iser is unintentionally ironic, because he argues there, in response to Stanley Fish, that it is inappropriate to extend the metaphor of text analysis to acts—a view not shared by Ricoeur, Taylor, or, apparently, Fish.

37. The extension of Program, Planning, and Budgetary Systems (PPBS) from the U.S. Department of Defense to various social policy arenas brought the language of target groups, delivery systems, and policy impacts to the realm of housing, health, education, and welfare. Much of the language of policy analysis is marked by this military metaphor—seeing clients as "targets," for instance—brought and introduced, perhaps, by Robert McNamara when he moved from the Department of Defense to the Ford Foundation, along with the PPBS that he brought with him. DeHaven-Smith (1988) has also noted the imagery of social policies as missiles. Criticisms of PPBS recapitulate the interpretivists' argument that the social world needs a science based on attributes of humans, rather than one based on the natural and physical worlds of trees and falling objects (whether apples or missiles).

38. Schutz (1967) referred to the first two dimensions as first and second order interpretations; Geertz (1983, p. 57) calls them experience-near and experience-distant. Van Maanen (1995, pp. 5-23) discusses the three "moments" of ethnography: collecting information, constructing a report, and its reading by several audiences.

39. See Hubbard (1989, p. 127) for an argument about the applicability of Heisenberg's uncertainty principle to social science.

40. Lather (1986) makes a similar argument, although not limited to policy analysis.

41. Pal refers to this as "localized information" (p. 203), specifically with respect to human rights abuses, his case example.

42. This is, in brief, the implication of the work of Schon and Rein (1994) and Roe (1994), as well as of essayists in Fischer and Forester (1993). I thank Michel van Eeten for this clarification.

43. See note 6.

2. ACCESSING LOCAL KNOWLEDGE: IDENTIFYING INTERPRETIVE COMMUNITIES AND POLICY ARTIFACTS

Getting started: that's the first concern of the policy analyst, as well as the researcher, and it is commonly addressed in methods texts under two headings: "entering the field" and "data collection." Most practicing policy analysts will already be in "the field" in some sense when they begin their research on a policy issue. If the analyst is on staff in a nonprofit organization or an implementing agency, or in a legislator's or a legislative committee's office, or working for a community group, she is already "in" that part of the field. She has entree to some actors by virtue of her position, and an official "excuse" to contact other actors in the policy field by virtue of her assignment.[1]

Once in the field, the researcher-analyst is concerned with what, in the scientific method, is called "data collection." Although appropriate for an experimental setting, the phrase is less apt for policy analysis, especially of an interpretive sort, as it implies that the data are or can be separated from their sources (much like butterfly specimens gathered for mounting); interpretive analysis requires that they be treated in their contexts. The "data" of interpretive analysis are the words, symbolic objects, and acts of policy-relevant actors along with policy texts, plus the meanings these artifacts have for them. These data remain in the possession of the actors after the researcher-analyst has gleaned them. What is "collected," if anything, are the researcher-analyst's observations and interpretations (taped, noted, or both) and copies of relevant documents.[2] In this sense, then, we might more properly speak of *accessing* the local knowledge that the analyst needs to make sense of a policy situation.

The purpose of the first steps in an interpretive policy analysis (assuming analytic assignment and entry have already been made) is twofold: to identify groups of people who might share understandings of policy ideas and language that would be different from other groups' understandings; and to identify the artifacts through which these understandings are expressed, communicated, and interpreted. These groups have been referred to variously as thought communities, speech or discourse communities, symbol-sharing communities, interpretive communities, and communities of practice. I use these terms interchangeably for the most part to signify groups that are not necessarily geographically based.[3] The policy or agency artifacts, or both, in the forms of language, objects, or acts, symbolically represent the meanings (values, beliefs, feelings) that the policy issue in question holds for various policy-relevant interpretive communities. The analyst needs to identify the artifacts as well as the groups for whom the artifacts have meaning, and what those meanings are.

Lawrence Vale (1998) is most reflective in commenting on the methods he used in analyzing policies concerning public housing project "redevelopment."[4] Although he does not use the language of interpretive communities and symbolically communicated meaning that I am developing here, these themes are clearly present in what he does say. In this case, "life in public housing" seems to be the artifact that is interpreted differently by different communities of meaning. Vale might have based an analysis on ideas expressed by Congress, the U.S. Department of Housing and Urban Development, or local government departments and agencies such as the Boston Housing Authority, or in interviews with planners and designers. Instead, by working through their tenant organizations, he accessed the local knowledge of residents in five Boston public housing developments. He hired and trained residents themselves as interviewers, paying them $10 an hour, an act that conveyed the message that their time was valued, as were, by implication, their viewpoints. "The tenants helped to shape the sorts of questions that were to be asked of their fellow residents, and encouraged me to find ways to raise issues that were important to them as well as to me" (Vale, 1998, p. 33). The result, he writes, was "267 hour-long taped interviews conducted in four languages that uncovered a broad range of tenant opinion at each development, reaching well beyond the realm of the usual activists and spokespersons" (p. 33). He acknowledges the logistical complexity of such a venture, as well as the "highly variable interviewing skills" of the resident researchers. But bringing this interpretive community's understandings of their lived experience to the table of policy discussions was worth the effort, Vale suggests: " . . . I still hold out hope that it marks at least a small attempt to counter the stereotypes still prevalent about public housing residents and their worlds" (p. 33).

The next three examples show not only the importance of accessing local knowledge, but how the identification of different interpretive communities and their discourses maps the architecture of issue debate. Linder's (1995) analysis of the EMF issue (discussed in Chapter 1) identified five interpretive communities and their associated discourses. Although he did not include a methods statement in the essay, one might infer from his endnotes, citations, and text that he attended public hearings and agency, community, and group meetings, read agency documents and newspaper accounts, and interviewed (and recorded, in notes or by tape, where appropriate) key actors, and from these identified the key words, objects, and acts used by various groups to communicate about EMF. In analyzing the written language of documents and his notes on, or tapes of, spoken language (from meetings, hearings, interviews), he discovered that the EMF power lines themselves were the artifact that held different meanings for different people. People who held different roles vis-à-vis the power lines (e.g., community residents, scientists, PUC members) tended to hold different interpretations of their meaning. Each group constituted, in this sense, an "interpretive community" or "community of meaning," which Linder discovered analytically: groups of people who articulated similar positions in their speech, writing, and acts with respect to the EMF issue (thought and speech communities, communities of practice). By analyzing how the talk about EMF and science differed across these data sources and groups, Linder was able to identify five different ways in which policy-relevant actors conceptualized "the" EMF problem and other associated matters (e.g., appropriate roles for governmental intervention).

Phyllis Chock (1995) provides another example, this one from hearings in the U.S. Congress on the subject of immigration. She identifies her sources in detail (p. 167), developing her analysis on the basis of transcripts of hearings and speeches in Congress between 1975 and 1986 and from publications of the U.S. Select Commission on Immigration and Refugee Policy. These allowed her to access the local knowledge of different policy-relevant publics in this case. In reading these transcripts she identified a term—"population"—that figured centrally in many speeches and discussions. Studying its use, she saw that it was understood and used differently by different speakers and writers: at different times it was used to mean "nations," "regions," "immigrants," or "ethnic groups." Her analysis of its usage, perhaps with the help of a good dictionary, traces the sources of the term to three conceptual origins—biology, nationalism, and business and sports.[5] Legislators using these three frames portrayed illegal immigrant "populations" as different from themselves. By contrast, speakers who were not legislators used the terms "persons" or "people." They told personal stories that gave agency to immigrants, portraying them as not so different from the speakers or their legislative audience. In this case, the different interpretive communities—for and against immigration—were fairly identifiable before analysis began; identification of significant linguistic artifacts and their conceptual entailments made clearer how they meant and understood different things in talking about what seemed to be the "same" subject and how these different conceptualizations would lead to different policies and programs.

A third example comes from Leslie Pal's (1995) analysis of the local knowledge held by Canadian nongovernmental organizations (NGOs) and the Canadian government with respect to United Nations human rights policy. Its liberal-democratic stance might lead observers to anticipate that the Canadian government and the NGOs would agree more than they would disagree—they are "part of a discourse coalition that shares a common belief system" (p. 187)—but in his analysis Pal shows that the "rights talk" engaged in by both shaped very different strategies and practices. In community terminology, both NGOs and government were members of the same community of belief but constituted different communities of practice. The artifact Pal focuses on is the language used in various forms, printed and oral, to talk about rights. Drawing on such documents as the Universal Declaration of Human Rights, various articles of the UN Charter, United Nations committee resolutions and draft resolutions, agency reports, minutes of meetings, letters, and memoranda, as well as notes and transcripts of comments made at meetings, interviews with NGO representatives and government officials, and observation of various meetings, Pal maps the architecture of the arguments of the various positions, and in this way shows which agencies join together in a discourse community. Like Linder and Chock, he details his sources but not his methods, but these details provide sufficient basis for inferring his analytic process in mapping the architecture of the arguments. In a fashion similar to Linder and Chock, he would have noted who said what, identified the words that appeared to carry significant meaning, noted what other ideas these entailed, and identified conflicting interpretations. (In the next chapter I present a more detailed example of this sort of language-focused analytic process.) Two communities of meaning emerge from his analysis, and it becomes clear that they differ in several dimensions: how actors see their roles and their notions of state sovereignty, what the purpose of the human rights debate is, the proper scope of debate, what constitutes acceptable evidence, and what action strategies to undertake. These are the dimensions that constitute the "architecture" of the argument, and each interpretive community understands its enactment differently. For example, government officials want documented evidence of human rights abuses, whereas NGOs accept anecdotal evidence based on the personal experience of informants under conditions that cannot easily be documented. Pal's analysis moves beyond analyzing differences of interpretation to showing how these link to differences of action, of practice.

These examples illustrate several of the steps in interpretive policy analysis.

1. The identification of communities of meaning or practice: groups of people who share a view of the policy issue under analysis (a more extended example of the process of discovering interpretive communities follows this section).

2. The identification of the specific artifacts (language, acts, objects) through which these views are expressed.

3. The mapping of the architecture of their similarities and differences with respect to the issue. These materialize in the way each group talks about the issue and in their actions with respect to it or the implications for action of that discourse.

This third step is related to what anthropologists describe as discovering the way the members of a group (tribe, profession, organization) categorize their social world. It is the knowledge of the definition of the situation used by members of the group to guide their thoughts, speech, and acts. It is the researcher-analyst's representation of their view of their world—their local knowledge, what the researcher-analyst would need to know to be a member of that world.[6]

Proceeding

Interviews, observation, and document analysis constitute the central interpretive methods for accessing local knowledge and identifying communities of meaning and their symbolic artifacts. Interpretive policy analysis often begins with *document analysis*, focusing initially on newspaper (and other media) coverage and extending to transcripts of committee hearings, various reports, legislation, or agency documents (depending on the policy issue and stage). These provide background information for *conversational interviews* with key actors (legislators, agency directors and staff, community members, representatives of interest groups) identified through these documentary sources and other interviews, in which the analyst's provisional assumptions about the boundaries of interpretive communities, the important artifacts, and their meanings can be corroborated or refuted. Persons interviewed are asked to suggest others with whom the analyst should talk, and interview transcripts (whether from notes or tapes) themselves then become sources for further analysis. Document analysis and conversational interviews may be preceded by or supplemented with *observation* of (with varying degrees of participation in) legislative debates, interest group meetings, implementing agencies, and community groups. When used together, these three methods are often referred to as *participant-observation* or *ethnography* (ethnographies traditionally present more cultural material than do participant-observations).[7]

These observational and interactive methods typically yield a set of notes —on settings, individuals, groups, agencies, interactions, patterns of activity, and so on—and perhaps also a stack of copies of documents. Some of these notes are daily logs that the researcher-analyst makes of his activities.

Some interpretive methodologists recommend keeping two diaries: one for recording observations of daily encounters, a second for personal responses to people, settings, and so on (Erlandson, Harris, Skipper, & Allen, 1993, pp. 143-145). Some of these notes are transcriptions made immediately following formal or informal interviews. With respect to the use of tape recorders during interviews, there are two opinions: do and don't. Those who argue against their use point out that tape recorders can interfere with the conversation: the person being interviewed becomes nervous when faced with a machine and a microphone; the interviewer is distracted by worry over tapes or batteries running out or operating the machinery; and researchers can train themselves to recall extended conversations and can transcribe the details immediately following the interview. Those who argue for the use of tape recorders maintain that people are, or quickly get, used to the presence of technological devices and that tape recorders alleviate researchers' worries over faulty memory. They also note, rightly in my view, that taking notes during a conversation interferes with its flow, diverting the interviewer's attention from what is being said.[8]

My own practice is to make a judgment based on the situation, with a bias against taping. A government official, for example, is more likely to be accustomed to having her words taped, a nonworking community resident less so. (The official may also say more if not on tape, but then the analyst has only his written record in case of disagreement.) I find taking notes and using a tape recorder equally intrusive. I have trained myself to be able to recall fairly clearly a 90-minute conversational interview, using an abbreviated topic outline that I follow during the conversation and jotting short notes or distinctive phrases occasionally during the interview.

Once one has a set of interview, observational, and document notes (or copies of documents), the process of directed, intensive analysis begins (as distinct from analyzing in the moment, or at the end of the day, while accessing data). Whatever analytic method one chooses (several are discussed in Chapters 3 through 5), all depend on an immersion in the details of these data. The researcher-analyst reads and rereads her notes. Some proceed by writing key ideas on note cards, one per card, noting the source of the words or observations; others rely on computer programs that accomplish the same task.[9] The cards, virtual or real, are shuffled and reshuffled by topic and outline, as analysis and report writing develop.

It is difficult to say how much time such a study takes, other than to observe that it is time-consuming (and paper-consuming: reporting the details of observational or conversational data typically takes much more space than numbers summarized in a table). It takes time to identify communities and key actors, to schedule and reschedule interviews, to observe, and to sift through agency archives and newspaper morgues. The level of government may affect the timetable: access may be easier and faster at local levels. The time required is certainly affected by the complexity of the policy issue and the number of agencies, groups, and levels of government involved. Under the time constraints (not to mention political, organizational, and other resource constraints) of workaday policy analysis, the comprehensive approach envisioned here may be more ideal than real (nevertheless, like the North Star, standing as a guide).

Although documents, especially newspapers (or their oral, audiovisual, and Internet equivalents), can be useful starting places, they are not the only sources. I have been using the term "community" to refer to people who share an interpretation of policy or implementing agency artifacts, without necessarily sharing the geographic basis that is the historical origin of the term. Sociology, especially community studies, and its related practices, social work and community organization, as well as the socially-aware design traditions of architecture, landscape architecture, and urban studies and planning, provide a neighborhood orientation for identifying communities. It can be useful to borrow their geographically-based methods, in addition to their terminology, for studying non-geographically-based communities. For an example I will draw on my own experience of getting started in a small town in Israel, analyzing the success of a national policy as implemented by local agencies created by the policy.[10]

Identifying Interpretive Communities in the Field:
An Example

The initial policy analytic question entailed identifying which community members used one of the local agencies (a community center), in what ways, which did not, and the reasons for both. I was hired as a community organizer, with one of the centers as my base. Because the policy was based on the rationale that using the center would improve the residents' quality of life, both the national agency and its local branches had an interest in increasing attendance.[11] To begin the research I "mapped" the "terrain" surrounding the community center. This meant walking the streets to get to know where the different social service, health, educational, and other public and nonprofit agencies were located, what sorts of people worked there, what characterized their services, and who did and did not attend. I was aided in this by a planning survey recently completed by the Ministries of the Interior and Housing and the Government Housing Corporation, which described not only the existing and projected physical layout (streets, sewerage, lighting, etc., and separation into residential, commercial, agricultural, and industrial zones) but also the town's history (including the history of its housing development) and its demographics (by age and country of origin) and employment picture. As I walked around, I noted differences in housing design, street "furniture," and image, and compared residential design with the design of public buildings, noting also internal differences among the latter (e.g., health clinics vs. city offices vs. labor union centers) and their contrast with commercial shops.[12]

At the same time I was also beginning to meet with people to talk about the town and its residents and what I had observed. Some of these conversational interviews were arranged in advance: I made appointments, for example, to meet with the community organizer in the welfare office, with school teachers and principals, with nurses at the well-baby clinics, with the heads of the local ministry offices of education, welfare, and recreation. I also arranged to meet with the mayor and vice-mayor, the heads of political parties, the Labor Union secretary, the heads of various women's and youth affiliates of the local political parties and labor organizations, and so on. In some cases, especially those with any political association, the community center director, my direct superior, arranged the meeting informally ahead of time and then walked me over to make the introduction. This located me organizationally for those with whom I was meeting: since I was newly arrived in town, I was an unknown in a place where residents had intimate knowledge of one another by family, place-of-origin, and political and religious affiliations. It also served to neutralize me from local politics: the community center was not affiliated with any party, and was determined to remain so. Having my boss introduce me clearly signaled that I was not plotting a coup by aligning myself (and through me, symbolically, the center) with one person and his party over another. In other cases, especially when dealing with counterparts in professional positions, I made the contact myself. Having an organizational association and a professional position was sufficient for these introductions. (These choices would be determined by the specifics of any particular context.)

I did not tape any of these conversational interviews. The machine would have been distracting, both to me and to others. Besides, I didn't want to lug it and the microphones and spare tapes and batteries around all day. I noted key phrases during the formal conversations, and transcribed from these and my memory as soon after each conversation as I could. I kept a daily log in which I recorded meetings, encounters, physical details, and other observations; I wrote my inferences, impressions, and feelings there, too, careful to identify these as such (that is, keeping observational and interview data separate from the inferences I made based on them). I was, at the same time, reading everything I could get hold of that described the town, its residents, its politics, its history. I asked people I interviewed if they had some brochure or document in their office that might give me useful background information on their agency, the town, or both. My newcomer status made this request commonplace for them. I received mostly agency documents and reports, some of them recent, some not, some done locally, some nationally or regionally. The only library sources I turned to were those that related the ideational and planning history of the type of town I was in, Israel's equivalent of Britain's "new towns." When copies were not available, I borrowed items and took notes before returning them.

As I began to be known among residents, I began to interview them as well. Most of these conversations were set up informally and in the moment, as I stopped at the greengrocers or other shops to buy lunch, posted letters, cashed checks, or stopped passersby on the street to ask for directions when I got lost. I also started to take part in community center activities, attending folk dancing classes, "hanging out" in the library (the lounge was more problematic: for gender reasons with the youth, and for gender, ethnic, and age reasons with the domino players), playing Ping-Pong, and so on. These activities created a context in which it was permissible for strangers to talk and for a newcomer to ask "obvious" and nosy questions. My notes and observations on these conversations went into my daily log.[13]

During these various observing, interviewing, and documenting excursions, I began to put together a picture of the various interpretive communities in the community center's environment. Some of these were apparent fairly quickly through observation, because age, ethnicity, profession, occupation, practice, or shared interest suggested a common interpretive perspective, corroborated by subsequent interviews. There were the group of Spanish Moroccan immigrant men who played dominoes in the center's lobby every afternoon, the teenagers who were bused to various regional high schools (there was none in the town) and who congregated in the center library in the afternoons and evenings, the unemployed young men who gathered in the center lounge in the late morning and then again in the evenings, and the staff at various agencies and town departments who thought that the center could assist (or interfere with or thwart) their work. Other groupings were identified by chance: the young father from a more remote neighborhood who came to ask the center director to set up activities near his home and turned out to be the spokesman for a larger group similar in age, background, and views; the three older women from a nearby village who came to borrow library books and decided they wanted to volunteer in the center and "volunteered" the services of their neighbors; and the two young men who, independently, came to offer to develop center programs, each of whom represented a different group of residents with different political affiliations and aspirations. The more I knew about the area in which residents lived, their countries of origin or heritage, and the schools their children attended, the more I knew about their social, religious, and political affiliations and socioeconomic status—the components in this context of different interpretive positions.

The artifacts around which these positions "danced" were the community center building and its programs, which I came to understand as symbols of identity and status (as a "stage" on which sociopolitical aspirations could be enacted and displayed and as a source of other resources in various forms—spaces for meetings, programs and classes, even budgets for various activities). In this instance I did not begin by reading town documents or newspapers—there was no local newspaper, and national newspapers provided only occasional coverage of town affairs (entirely crisis- or scandal-oriented)—but rather by "reading" the spatial and interorganizational environment of the implementing agency. These observations, and the documents that I subsequently started reading, gave me background material for the interviews I conducted.

I took these notes and copies "home," to my office desk. I read and reread them, and out of this increasing familiarity I began to see patterns and connections. This analytic process yielded a conceptual topic outline (which went through several revisions as analysis and writing proceeded). I transferred quotes, observational details, and inferences to note cards and arranged them according to the outline, carefully noting the source of each. (This was long before anyone had a personal computer, let alone a program to do this sort of process, but even today I prefer the note card method: I need to be able to pile the cards on my desk, hold them physically, and shuffle them around.) Working from this arrangement of the cards, I prepared the first draft of my analytic report. This report was presented to the center director and the area community organization coordinator, and served as a guide to subsequent policy and program development. A subsequent research project concerned the role of community organizers in the agency. For this analysis I could build on earlier participant-observation, interviewing, and document analysis, adding further interviewing and document study directed specifically toward this question. In this case, where I discovered in preparing the report that I needed additional information, I could contact people I had already interviewed for follow-up conversations. This analysis was commissioned by an independent funding agency that had underwritten community organization programs for several years. I presented the report to a panel of program heads from the agency. The discussion was lively, but in this case I do not know what effect, if any, the report had on their thinking.

Such a community-based study is an example of perhaps the most extensive and varied use of forms of interpretive analysis. Other analyses, which are agency- or issue-directed, may be more narrow in scope. It is a good example, however, of the range of activities and contacts that constitute interpretive analyses.

Summary: Identifying Communities; Sources of Data

Interpretive communities arise around a shared point of view relative to a policy issue. What that point of view will be in any situation will depend on the policy in question, but some common points of beginning reference are those factors according to which a society or polity categorizes itself: race-ethnicity, class, age, religion, political ideology, professional or occupational experience, hobbies or pastimes, and so on. These are manifested in many ways: the researcher-analyst might look for people spending time together or working in the same organizational area or having similar training, or he might simply look for people who read the same newspaper (when there is a choice of more than one). Observing what people do and how they do it, listening to how they talk about the issue, reading what they read, and talking with them about their views will lead the analyst to a degree of familiarity with the issue and views on it from the perspective of those affected by it in whatever way. Out of this growing familiarity, the researcher-analyst will be able to identify the overlappings and commonalities that will begin to define borders between communities of different interpretive positions.

Depending on the specific policy and the analysis, sources of local knowledge may include:

1. Written Sources
    a. news accounts (from newspapers, radio, television, magazines, journals). These provide background on the issue and can help identify policy-relevant actors, both individuals and groups (such as interest groups, community groups, or agencies).

b. agency newsletters, annual reports, memos, correspondence, meeting protocols, notes

c. government documents, hearings testimonies, reports, surveys, and other studies

Note: Any of these may be found in archives containing past years' records as well as in current files.

2. Oral Sources: interviews with key actors and members of other policy-relevant groups and individuals. Develop a map of key actors by asking, With whom else should I be speaking?

3. Observation

a. of acts and interactions (with whom do people speak and not speak? who spends time where, and with whom? who doesn't go where, and why?)

b. of objects (e.g., the design of agency buildings and other built spaces, laundry hanging from lines, the posture, clothing, or other characteristics of people on the street or in the agency)

4. Participation: in the lived experience of agency or community members, or both, as relevant to the specific analysis.

These are summarized in Table 2.1. The analyst should use several sources of data, as if she were building a Picasso-like portrait of an organizational or community or policy "face" from multiple angles. In this way, the analyst attempts to see the issue and its meanings from as many angles as possible.

As policy analysts begin to access local knowledge, they also begin the process of analyzing it. The interpretive policy analyst needs to build a context in which to access local knowledge. Knowing what specific object or piece of language has significance comes from situational familiarity— understanding what is important to stakeholders, to policy-relevant publics. This is gained through the activities associated with site- or field-based research (participant-observation, ethnography): observing, talking, interacting, interviewing, and reading. These provide a set of observations (in the broadest sense) for further analysis. The process entails two phases: (1) a daily sensemaking, out of which (2) puzzles emerge (events or acts or interactions that contradict what the analyst expected, or which he cannot make sense of, given what he knows at that moment, or which contradict one another).

In attempting to make sense of these puzzles or anomalies, the analyst may draw on specific tools or techniques for assistance. As aids to clearer thinking, they are methods of exploring data that the researcher already "has" and that he usually has already begun to make sense of, to interpret. The tools enable a process of making these insights and understandings more explicit. In traditional methods texts these two processes are typically

Table 2.1 Accessing Local Knowledge

Methods of Accessing Data	Sources of Data	Kinds of Data Yielded
Observing	Meetings Legislative sessions Agency programs, acts	Acts Interactions Nonverbal language Uses of objects
Conversational interviewing	Various policy stakeholders	Spoken language Nonverbal language
Document analysis	Archives, files Memos, letters, notes Annual reports Surveys, studies Newspapers, journals	Written language Descriptions of objects Historical records of events, acts, interactions
Participant-observation, ethnography	Implementing agency programs, offices Legislature, local government Community groups Interest groups	All of the above

separated under the headings "data collection" and "data analysis," although often they are neither conducted separately in time nor separable in analysis. While the analyst is in the process of interviewing, for instance, he is often analyzing as well. Yet there comes a time when the analyst feels that all key people have been interviewed and interpretive communities identified (no new names are offered when the analyst asks, "With whom else should I speak?" and he feels that the policy debate has been fully mapped). At this point, after data have been accessed, many formal methods may be engaged, often after the analyst is no longer physically at the site that was the source of local knowledge. The next three chapters consider some of these analytic methods.

NOTES

1. I will not expand further on this subject, about which much has been written in community and organizational contexts. See Spradley and McCurdy (1972), Whyte (1984), or Murphy (1980) for starters.

2. I am eliding here the question of whether the data are the artifacts and their meanings, or the researcher's interpretations of those artifacts and what he is told they mean. In my own view, a researcher-analyst is always dealing with interpretations and "interpretations of interpretations," in Geertz's (1973) phrase: data of any sort cannot be perceived except through some organizing conceptual lens, although with some things (the length of an inch, the meaning of these words) the consensus about their interpretation is so widespread that we are no longer aware of the interpretive acts underlying their naming and comprehension.

3. The sources for two of these terms are Black (1962, p. 40: speech community) and Lave and Wenger (1991: communities of practice). The others are fairly commonly used. The terms appear to differ not only along disciplinary lines—the language philosopher Black focusing on speech, educational scholars Lave and Wenger focusing on learning— but also on their relative emphasis on cognition. "Symbol-sharing communities," "interpretive communities," and "communities of practice" seem to move further and further in developing the conceptual link of cognition with action. Black is interesting in this regard, laying a foundation for that link. His concern was how metaphors might be understood as part of public discourse, rather than private musings, and he wrote: their literal meanings must be part of a shared context—"a set of standard beliefs . . . ([or] current platitudes) that are the common possession of the members of some speech community" (1962, p. 40).

4. These comments were made on the occasion of receiving an award for the article, "Empathological places: Residents' ambivalence toward remaining in public housing," (1997), *Journal of Planning Education and Research, 16,* 159-175. The article does not include a reflective methodology, although Vale is apparently preparing such an essay.

5. She, too, is not this explicit about her precise methods of analysis, writing to an audience she assumes shares her approach. The reference to a "good" dictionary is not facetious: the *American Heritage Dictionary* and the *Oxford English Dictionary* are better sources of a word's conceptual origins than are others.

6. See, e.g., Spradley and McCurdy 1972, especially chapters 1, 2, and 4. This is also the language of ethnomethodology (the "definition of the situation"); see Garfinkel (1977).

7. The literature on each of these is vast. The following are some representative sources. On interviewing, see Holstein and Gubrium (1995, pp. 38-51, 73-80), Spradley and McCurdy (1972, pp. 41-56), and Whyte (1984, pp. 97-127). On observing see Spradley and McCurdy (1972, chap. 4) and Whyte (1984, pp. 83-96). On document analysis, observing, and interviewing, see Murphy (1980). The classic methodological description of "fieldwork"—accessing local knowledge—is Whyte's appendix to the second edition (1955) of his 1943 work. For a discussion of theoretical concerns, see Geertz (1973). Gans (1976) provides an insightful reflection on the conduct of partici- pant-observation and the continuum of roles between observer and participant.

8. See Erlandson et al., 1993, pp. 90-91; Murphy, 1980, pp. 85-87; and Whyte, 1984, pp. 113-115, for discussions of these views.

9. NUD•IST (distributed by Sage/Scolari) is one such program.

10. This is presented at length in Yanow (1996b). My initial intention was to learn something about "being an Israeli," out of personal interest. As theoretical issues emerged, the research and analysis became the basis for my dissertation research.

11. There were good organizational reasons for this interest as well: higher attendance figures proved the success of the agency, which translated into increased funding and ongoing political support. The analysis was designed as a long-term project, and analytic and intervention phases were not clearly demarcated. The research question constituted one of the sometimes explicit, sometimes implicit rationales for the central agency's creation of an internal community organization (CO) unit and an initial dozen CO positions. I have developed these arguments elsewhere (Yanow, 1996b).

12. On the design of the "street," see Appleyard (1981), Halprin (1972), and Lynch (1960, 1972). On the relationship between urban design elements and meaning, see Jackson (1980), Meinig (1979), and Tuan (1977). See also the notes in Chapter 4.

13. My students often ask, and so perhaps I should note here: these conversations took place in Hebrew, which is one of Israel's three official languages (Arabic and English being the other two) and the common language of most of its residents (many of whom also speak at least one other language). I had mastered enough before beginning this project to be able to converse fairly fluently, albeit somewhat more slowly at first; my speed and proficiency in contemporary and local slang, as well as my reading ability, increased rapidly with use.

3. SYMBOLIC LANGUAGE

Interpretive analyses consider a wide range of language, including not only the written language of the policy itself but also the spoken and written language of committee debates and testimony, implementing agencies' multiple forms of documents (annual reports, correspondence, etc.), and interviews. This chapter focuses on two specific methods of analyzing language in search of policy meanings—metaphor analysis and category analysis—and concludes with an overview of the developing narrative approaches to policy analysis that have recently emerged.

Metaphor Analysis[1]

What a "community center" in the context of an Israeli development town would be was something the agency's founding Board of Directors spent a good bit of time exploring. One day, one of the directors sitting around the table at a board meeting said, "The community center will be a 'functional supermarket.'"

This bit of organizational storytelling is paraphrased, except for the direct quote, from the words of Dr. Ya'el Pozner, a member of the first Board of Directors, and later an officer of the Israel Corporation of Community

Centers (ICCC). In our interview (in the fall of 1979), she proceeded to tell me about the founding of the agency created by national legislation to enact a major social policy—how the directors shaped the idea of what a community center would be, what programs it would have, what its physical plant would look like. I had already encountered the phrase—the community center as "functional supermarket"—in agency literature and in other interviews, as well as in the course of participant-observation in the early 1970s, and it had seemed as natural and as reasonable as any other way of describing a community center. Following our interview, however, as I transcribed and reflected on my notes, I found myself thinking of it as an "unnatural" phrase. I wondered, In what way or ways *is* a "community center" like a "supermarket"?

This is an example of an organizational metaphor that carried policy meanings. To begin to understand what it meant in this organizational and policy context, we need to understand something of metaphors. What exactly a metaphor is, and how it works, has long been the subject of debate in circles of philosophy, linguistics, psychology, and literary theory.[2] Drawing on some of this debate, we can define metaphor as the juxtaposition of two superficially unlike elements (in technical terms, the "vehicle" or source and the "focus") in a single context, where the separately understood meanings of both interact to create a new perception of the focus of the metaphor (and sometimes of the vehicle as well). Subjected to analysis, the surface unlikeness yields to a set of characteristics found in both metaphoric vehicle and focus. For example, most would agree that "black" and "day" have little in common. Yet in the phrase "It was a black day for the Red Sox," attributes associated with "blackness"—darkness, disaster, misfortune— are transferred to "day" through the juxtaposition, and we infer that the team lost the ball game, probably through some player's error or other mishap (the concatenation of darkness with daylight capturing the often found ironic posture common to diehard Red Sox fans).

The contemporary equivalent of the Greek etymology of the word— *metapherein*—is a moving van, and we can see metaphoric meaning being moved by and through the "vehicle" or source to its focus. This metaphoric process of transferring meaning from a better known entity to a lesser known entity characterizes several language forms other than metaphor proper: analogy, translation, exchange, contradiction, synecdoche, and metonymy (Miller, 1982, 1985). It is, as Lakoff and Johnson (1980) note, a common mode of learning: we begin with what we know and transfer that understanding to something unknown.

Metaphor has long been treated as a figure of speech or literary device that reflects imprecise thinking. Since as long ago as Plato and Aristotle, metaphoric language has been contrasted with literal language. According to the prevailing theory, metaphoric language was the inferior of the two (being less precise, less scientific, appealing to the emotions, and so forth) and could be eliminated, leaving only literal figures. More recent developments in cognitive linguistics treat metaphor more as a way of seeing or learning, and as such, as an elemental part of language and thought, rather than as decoration that can be eliminated. As Lakoff and Johnson (1987) wrote,

> Metaphor is not a harmless exercise in naming. It is one of the principal means by which we understand our experience and reason on the basis of that understanding. To the extent that we act on our reasoning, metaphor plays a role in the creation of reality. (p. 79)

Although metaphors may initially appear to be merely descriptive, outside the world of literature—in organizational and policy practices—they often acquire a prescriptive aspect. Metaphors no longer only present new insights into the situations they describe: they also suggest possible action in response to those situations. Metaphors may express some prior, unarticulated understanding of the situation. That is, metaphors can be both models *of* a situation and models *for* it.[3] Attuned to the fact that we use metaphoric language not just in poetry but in daily speech, including organizational and policy speech, and that metaphoric language shapes action as well as thought, the policy analyst can begin to attend to the metaphoric nature of such policy phrases noted earlier (see Chapter 1) as "housing decay" (from tooth decay) or "broken homes" (parallel to "broken china"), with their attendant implications for an appropriate "reparative" role for governmental intervention: call in the "housing doctor" to yank out the offending construction, glue the family back together. Uncovering the metaphoric roots of policy or agency language and acts is one way of discovering the architecture of the policy argument.

Our working definition of metaphor, together with the philosophical position that underlies an interpretive approach, leads to the following analytic steps, illustrated by the "community center as supermarket." The first step is to identify the conceptualizations used by policy-relevant actors. "Supermarket" was a concept introduced by agency founders; it eventually spread through the agency and came to be used by center directors, community organizers, and other personnel. In the field research setting, the metaphor was like a "found object": it was there in speech, showing up in interviews and in conversations, and it appeared in printed materials—in agency memos and correspondence, as well as in annual reports. When the researcher-analyst introduces metaphoric language, it should be an articulation of the local knowledge of policy-relevant actors and groups.

Once we have identified a policy or organizational metaphor in actors' language or thinking, we can begin the task of deciphering its meaning in their frame of reference. We would, in this case, ask: What are the characteristics of a supermarket, the "vehicle" of the metaphor? But it cannot be any supermarket: it has to be a supermarket in Israel. And it cannot be a supermarket in Israel in 1999: it has to be a supermarket in Israel in the late 1960s to early 1970s, at the time that the board member made this metaphoric comparison and it entered agency speech. In other words, the researcher-analyst's elaboration of the entailments of the metaphor—the denotations and connotations of its source—must be grounded in the context (both setting and time) out of which it grew.

The next analytic question makes explicit the implied comparison: In what way or ways is the focus of the metaphor (the community center as it took shape) like the vehicle or source of the metaphor (a circa 1970 Israeli supermarket)? Where in the community center do the supermarket features that we have just identified appear? What in community center design, practices, or both is reminiscent of these attributes of a supermarket? The researcher-analyst might ask, during a conversational interview, "What did (does) it mean (to you) to think of the community center as a supermarket?" In this way, she begins to spell out the usually tacitly known local meaning of what makes a supermarket and the ways in which a community center might be like one. Analysis draws on insights into local knowledge gained from prior observation, participation, document study, and/or interviews.[4]

In the process of clarifying the meanings within the local lexicon of both the vehicle (supermarket) and the focus (community center) of the metaphor, it often helps to think alternately of one, then the other. Just as aspects of supermarkets clarify the community center concept, so aspects of the community center bring out the tacitly known elements that constitute a supermarket. It may also help the analysis to identify a contrasting case within the local context of meaning, in relation to the metaphoric source. In this example, it became clear, from observing supermarkets and the locations where community centers were established and from reading agency members' descriptions of them, that the supermarket in Israel of the late 1960s stood in sharp contrast to two other types of institutions that sold

Table 3.1 Supermarkets and Not-Supermarkets: A Comparative Analysis

Supermarket	Shuk	Makolet
Building		
big	none (open air wood stalls)	small
chain	local	family store
Merchandise		
wide range	mostly limited to produce, baked goods, fish, fowl, meat (limited or no canned, bottled, or paper goods)	limited range
variety within type	seasonal variety	limited selection
pre-packaged	loose	some of each
high quality	variable	produce not as fresh
Style		
fixed prices	bargaining, haggling	fixed prices
formal credit arrangements	no credit	personal credit
clean, brightly lit, orderly	disarray	orderly, dimly lit, not sparkling
modern/Western (U.S.)	Eastern/Levantine	Old World

food: the open-air market (the *shuk*) and the corner grocery store (the *makolet*). By making the differences explicit—in terms of local knowledge, in what ways is the supermarket *not* a shuk or a makolet?—the elements that the former brought to the community center become clearer. These comparisons are presented in Table 3.1.

Bringing this form of analysis to bear on the interview, written and observational data led to the following sensemaking. The metaphor articulated a specific design context—especially in terms of size and mass—within which community center buildings could be envisioned; it created a sense of what community center programs should include, in terms of their variety and scope; it included ideas about measures of success; and it suggested appropriate roles for staff and expectations for clients' behavior. These enacted policy ideas.

The sense of the metaphor, as used by founders, administrators, and staff, in interviews and in writing, was that the community center would be a multifaceted facility providing a wide variety of programs at the local level, programs that supposedly were not already locally available to residents commercially or through other agencies. Just as a supermarket offers a seemingly endless variety of standardized merchandise all in one place to a broad range of consumers, the community center would "meet the maximum number of desires expressed by residents for programmatic activities," in the words of one of the ICCC's brochures. Just as the Israeli supermarket of the 1960s and 1970s, as an ideal-typical concept, is a large, centrally located, spacious building providing many goods under one roof, the ideal community center would similarly be large, spacious, and central. It would contain space for many activities: theatrical and musical performances and classes, a library and an espresso bar, photography classes, and football tournaments. New community center buildings themselves, although not identical, had design features common to supermarkets and different from other local buildings, such as their large scale and sense of expansiveness. They had high ceilings, large rooms, and often two floors, were typically located on or adjacent to the central town or neighborhood plaza, and were markedly distinct from both public and private local architecture.

Metaphoric analysis also generated concepts, categories, or "labels" from supermarket language, which accurately describe the ICCC and its activities. For example, the community center would offer a full array of "prepackaged goods": programs, activities, and clubs running the gamut from sports to crafts, from remedial education to music and dance. These would be created and designed by agency staff, often at the national office, based on their own ideas (rather than in response to local requests) and offered "ready-made" to those who would sign up. The metaphor placed a value on the "high turnover of goods": large numbers of local residents participating in a wide variety of activities. Local residents would develop "shopping lists" of what they would like to "buy" in the community center and communicate this to the director, who would "stock" his shop with program "supplies" from various Ministry departments, "advertise" his "wares" in the neighborhood, and wait for "customers" to sign up.

In addition to shaping thought and action about building design and program offerings, the supermarket metaphor also guided thought and action about administrative practices and staff roles. These expectations could be seen in agency evaluation forms and in ways in which directors and staff talked about their work (although only a few referred explicitly to the supermarket metaphor). Community centers were evaluated on their "volume of sales": the higher the attendance and membership figures and the greater the number of programs and activities offered, the more successful the community center was thought to be. Like a supermarket manager, the community center director would be on hand in his office for client-

Table 3.2 Supermarkets and Community Centers: A Metaphoric Analysis

Supermarket	Community Center
Building	
High-ceilinged, large	Spacious
Capacious	Multifaceted facility
Accessible	Centrally located
Chain	Local site of national agency
Merchandise/Programs	
Wide variety	Range of choices
Pre-packaged	Largely developed nationally
High quality	High quality in concept
Staff roles	
In store	Community organizers in neighborhoods; other personnel in house
Sales	"Selling" programs
Customer relations	
Fixed prices	Price list for membership, classes
Credit available	Formal payment arrangements
Evaluation criteria	
# of customers	# of members, clients, participants in programs
# of sales, turnover rate of goods	# of memberships taken out, classes registered for

customers to come inside the building to "shop" for available "products" and to request others. Community center staff—sports directors, adult education coordinators, children's activities programmers, librarians, and so forth—were cast in the role of "sales clerks" or "cashiers." They were expected to be available to clients inside the building and to promote the standardized activities of the community center. When community organizers hired by the ICCC did not follow these role expectations—they worked outside the buildings in the neighborhoods, following the tenets of their professional training—conflict developed.[5] The comparative analysis is summarized in Table 3.2.

Metaphoric meaning presupposes an understanding of the literal sense in some context. If we did not know the ordinary local meaning of "supermarket," we could not apply it sensibly to ICCC community centers. For metaphors to be understood in public discourse (rather than as private images), their source meanings must be part of a shared context: "a set of standard beliefs . . . that are the common possession of the members of some speech community" (Black, 1962, p. 40)—or community of thought, of interpretation, of practice.

The supermarket phrase was soon picked up throughout the agency. This is what made it a public, "organizational" metaphor: it entered the oral and written discourse (including practices) of the organization. Dr. Pozner recalled in an interview that her early planning committee, which had been charged with inventing the model community center, tried to design a building that would be a "functional supermarket" in that it would meet the largest possible number of residents' wishes: it would contain space for performances and sports, for different clubs or classes, as well as a "members' lounge" (Lavi, 1979). The ICCC's 1974-75 Annual Report referred to the community center as a "supermarket of ideas and programs for all ages, at all levels." The metaphor appears in subsequent years in documents and conversations as a "supermarket of classes" and a "supermarket of services." A center director referred to herself and her colleagues, in 1980, as "supermarket 'owners' or 'clerks'." The metaphor became the shared understanding of the thought, speech, and practice community that was the ICCC at that time and shaped a variety of actions taken in implementing its enabling legislation.

Further analysis reveals that the link between the American background of supermarkets and the American background of community centers was important for the communication of a set of policy meanings that figured elsewhere in the policy issue. The possibility that metaphoric meaning reflects broader societal cultural meaning(s) appears also in other analyses. McCoy (1995, chap. 4), for example, analyzes the program name "ecological agriculture" in the context of Chinese-U.S. international policy in the early 1990s, identifying it as a metaphor that reflected cultural thinking about and action with respect to agriculture. He proceeds by asking what "agriculture" means to the Chinese and to the West and comparing the two.

In playing out the metaphoric analysis, the analyst will discover how much of the policy issue it explains and whether metaphoric entailments are recapitulated in other arenas of policy or agency acts. The wider the "echoes" or "ripples" of metaphoric meaning, the more robust the analysis and the more likely that it will help articulate the architecture of the policy argument.

Category Analysis[6]

As they identify and name groups of people on whose behalf governmental action is sought, public policies often create sets of categories and labels or invoke and reflect category structures already in use in a polity. The relationship is complex: category authorship cannot always be established clearly. The language in question, then, is at times less the "found object" bounded by an agency, program, or policy "site" that organizational metaphors may be, and more the language of general discourse. Such is the case with the categories in use in the United States today, when talking about racial and ethnic groups: they are found in policy and agency language, but they are also widespread in common usage. This is an example of a situation in which the categories of policy discourse and the formal categories of the policy issue itself overlap. In conducting an analysis of contemporary American uses of "race," "ethnicity," and their associated categories, I was interested in what people using race-ethnic terms and concepts mean, as these meanings are reflected in and shaped by policy and administrative practices. I sought to map the architecture of meaning underlying the formal categories, because these practices and meanings undergird some currently highly contested policy issues (e.g., affirmative action) in the United States. Any attempt to revise or reform these policies will have to engage these meanings.

In such a study, interpretive analysis is still trying to "read" the meanings that policy-relevant actors—in this case, a much larger set of groups than in the ICCC case—have vested in the categories, rather than the meanings they hold for the researcher-analyst or their a priori social science meanings. Here, policy-relevant actors include the legislators and policymakers who created policies for the Equal Employment Opportunity Commission (EEOC), the Census Bureau, and other programs and agencies that collect race-ethnic data, as well as agency administrators and other personnel involved with category definition and data collection and members of the public who belong to, find their identity in, and contest those categories.

Categories entail and reflect a set of ideas about their subject matter. By making a close "reading" of the categories a society collectively constructs in and through its public policies and administrative practices, the policy analyst can make those ideas more explicit, not as espoused, but as enacted, reflecting the collective or social dimension of category and concept construction, learning, and knowing. Categories, by commonsense definition, highlight elements deemed similar within the boundaries they draw and different from elements beyond those boundaries. These samenesses of things within categories and differences between things in different categories become the organizing principles around which categories are built: something belongs in Category A because it shares "A-ness" and is not "not-A." The cognitive organizing principles underlying category-making are typically not made explicit, although this knowledge is known, usually tacitly, to members of the group (organization, community, polity, tribe) creating and using the categories (and it is passed on, also usually as tacit knowledge, to new members). Members of a community have the ability to, and typically do, group objects into similarity sets without having to ask, or needing an answer to, "similar with respect to what?" Category analysis makes both that question and its answers explicit, in identifying what the samenesses and differences are. This is the architecture of meaning underlying the categories.

Categories constitute sets, which share the features with respect to which of their elements are the same and different; the so-called basic food groups, for example, share "food-ness." A category and its contents are internally undifferentiated—they constitute a single unit, a whole—while also being perceived as clearly distinct from all other categories and their contents in the category set. At the same time, their structuring blinds us to other features (by definition, not moral failure) that nonetheless remain present in the categorized elements. Meat, fish, eggs, and yogurt, divided by one schema into two categories, are all animal "products," although this singular grouping, too, is occluded by yet another category set organized from a different point of view (one that categorizes, for example, by meat flesh, fish flesh, non-meat-or-fish-flesh, and dairy). The highlighting of some features lends them, on the surface, an importance denied to the occluded features. The conceptual logic of category-making implies that the differences between members of different categories are sharp, when from another viewpoint they may be only minor gradations of difference.

Furthermore, when a single category is treated, the similarities of its elements become more central than their differences from elements of other categories. But when a set of categories is examined, it is the differences that become most important. Classifying entails an interpretive choice on the basis of a decision about the relative importance of certain features over others. The analyst needs to attend not only to what characteristics are being highlighted as the basis for category-making, but also to which ones are being obscured or occluded. Since we are looking at a *social* construction in the public sector, analysis needs to ask, Is our category-making contributing to silences in our public discourse? (I take this idea further in Chapter 5.)

A set of category names or labels implies two sorts of things about the world of elements being categorized. First, the names or labels suggest that nothing has been left out: the categories are exhaustive, and everything in the category world has a place in one of the categories. Second, there is no overlap in category membership: the categories are discrete, and no element fits into more than one category. Categories become problematic when either (or both) of these two principles is violated: when one or more elements don't fit, or when one element fits into more than one category. Tacit knowledge is also present in the treatment of some elements as the "normal" or usual case, from which the others are deviations. The latter are referred to as "marked" categories—for example, woman doctor, or Asian American actor. Here, "doctor" and "actor" are the "unmarked" cases, the "default values," so to speak, the expected norms. The unmarked case is often taken to be the more basic variety, the simpler version, at times connoting a "better" one. The marked case is treated as different, not normal, which in contemporary American culture often connotes an inferior version.[7]

To summarize, category analysis asks:

1. What are the categories being used in this policy issue?
2. What do elements have in common that makes them belong together in a single category? Does categorical logic depend on one or more markings?
3. What, if any, elements do not fit, or does one (or more) appear to fit more than one category? Why (what are their characteristics, and how do these compare with the characteristics of the fitting elements)?
4. Do the elements as they are used in policy practices signal different meanings of category labels than what the category labels themselves appear to mean?
5. Is there a point of view from which those things implicitly asserted as belonging together are or could be seen as divergent?

I began analysis with the policy instrument that uses race and ethnicity most extensively: the U.S. Census in its most recent version. (I have extended the analysis to other policies and practices using the concepts and categories, but will restrict the discussion here to the census.) I identified the questions in the 1990 census that asked explicitly about race and ethnicity and about related matters:

Question 4 asks: "What is . . .'s race?"
Question 7 asks: "Is . . . of Spanish/Hispanic origin?"
Question 13 asks: "What is this person's ancestry or ethnic origin?"
And *Question 15* asks, "Does this person speak a language other than English at home?"[8]

The existence of separate questions for race, Spanish/Hispanic origin, and ancestry or ethnic origin implied that these had separate meanings: race and ethnicity were seemingly separate categories, and Spanish/Hispanic origin was being treated as different from ethnic origin. The separate usage of race and ethnicity is in keeping with the common sense of race as denoting physical characteristics (especially of face, hair, and skin) and ethnicity as denoting cultural characteristics (such as foods, clothing, language, religion, and history). The next step of the analysis was to see whether the analytic categories used for Questions 4 and 13 maintained this distinction. The analytic categories appear in three places: on the census questionnaire itself (as examples for the person reading and filling in the form), in instructions to the census taker, and in Census Bureau reports. The answer block printed on the census form provides for the following answers for Question 4 (race):

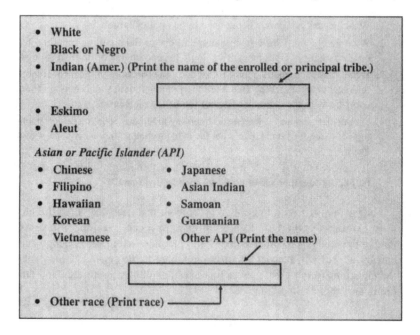

The subcategories White, Black or Negro, American Indian, and Asian or Pacific Islander appear, on the surface, to fit into the category "race" as it and they are used in the United States today. However, the sub-subcategories for Asian and Pacific Islander are not races (again, as that term is used today: Chinese and Samoans do not share facial or skin characteristics) but refer to nation-states. Eskimo and Aleut are also not races, but "peoples"

or ethnic groups, bearing some categorical similarity to American Indian tribes (although they are listed separately because they argued that they are not, historically speaking, American Indians).[9] This means that the category "race" is being used to mean something other than physical characteristics. This is borne out further in the instructions to the census taker, which offer the following possibilities for "Other API": Cambodian, Tongan, Laotian, Hmong, Thai, Pakistani, and so on. These are also nation-states, with the exception of the Hmong, who are a people or ethnic group, as that is commonly understood. Furthermore, the Census Bureau's analysis of the data includes the following additional groups:

Asian	*Pacific Islander*
Bangladeshi	Tahitian
Burmese	North Mariana Islander
Indonesian	Palavan
Malayan	Fijian
Okinawan	Other
Sri Lankan	
Other	

These, too, are references to states rather than to races.

For Question 13 (ancestry or ethnic origin), the census form offers the following as possibilities: "German, Italian, Afro-American, Croatian, Cape Verdean, Dominican, Ecuadoran, Haitian, Cajun, French Canadian, Jamaican, Korean, Lebanese, Mexican, Nigerian, Irish, Polish, Slovak, Taiwanese, Thai, Ukrainian etc." Most of these are also references to nation-states, with three exceptions: Afro-American, Cajun, and French Canadian, categories of people who share, in varying degrees, a history, food customs, music, and language. (In 1990 Croatian was also a cultural, rather than national, grouping.) Among the states listed are some—Lebanese, Irish—which themselves include different ethnic heritages as that term is commonly understood—Christian and Muslim in Lebanon, Catholic and Protestant in Ireland. In other words, ethnicity and race are not being used as if they had distinct meanings.

This is underscored by the treatment of subcategories in Question 7 (Spanish/Hispanic origin). The census form offers the following as possible answers to the respondent answering in the affirmative:

> Mexican, Mexican-American, Chicano
> Puerto Rican
> Cuban
> Other

Instructions given to the census taker about "Other" identify "Argentinian, Colombian, Dominican, Nicaraguan, Salvadoran, Spaniard, and so on" as possibilities. These, too, treat origin as nationality, raising the question of how this national origin differs from national origin as ethnicity (Question 13), or national origin as race (Question 4). Interestingly, individuals are allowed to self-identify in the 1990 census (the enumerator is instructed, "If response is 'Other race,' ask—Which group does . . . consider (himself/ herself) to be?"), unlike in EEOC policy (where the employer is to identify employees without asking them, according to how they would be perceived in the community), raising questions about the extent to which physical ("racial") features are identifiable. But mixed race self-identity is not allowed: the census taker is instructed, "Fill ONE circle for the race that the person considers himself/herself to be" (although this is to change in Census 2000).

In studying categories and subcategories, the analyst is asking, What are the characteristics of the labels? What do they mean at the particular time and place of their usage? What do they have in common that makes them "belong" to one set of categories, and to only one category within the set, rather than to another category or to another set (e.g., what in the answers to Question 4 means "race," to Question 7 means "ethnicity or cultural heritage," and to Question 13 means "Hispanic"; and in what ways are they different, such that "race" means something different from "ethnicity")? The overarching approach is the same as the one used in analyzing metaphors: once we identify the particular language of policy-relevant actors, what are the context-specific meanings that that language has for those actors?

The analytic step of comparing and contrasting to sharpen analysis, although identical in concept to metaphor analysis, is different here. In metaphor analysis, the contrast is usually unstated in the context and is introduced by the analyst, drawing on knowledge of the context (e.g., the *shuk* and *makolet,* by comparison with which the supermarket was exciting, new, and different).[10] In category analysis, the contrast is usually present in the set of category labels, because the conceptual meaning of categorization lies in comparison and contrast with other categories in the category set and with the members of those categories. In both cases, the analyst draws out the contrasting meanings.

Here, the census questions pointed to two contrasting category labels, "race" and "ethnicity," as well as to two other potentially contrasting cases of "Hispanic" and "language." Census forms and published Census Bureau accounts provided a long list of member elements for each category. Studying member elements revealed three organizing principles according to which they could be grouped together ("similar with respect to what?"). Some were geographic place names, either nation-states (Italian, French, Argentinian) or continents (African American, Asian American). Others were colors: white, black. And a third group was "cultures" as that word is understood to mean a shared history (Afro-Americans), a shared language (French Canadians, Hispanics), or a "people" in the sense of "tribe" (Hmong). But in actual use by the Census Bureau, these three dimensions were present in both the "race" and the "ethnicity" questions: race and ethnicity did not mean two different things in practice. Category membership rules were blurred.

On further analysis, it became clear that groups that were asserted implicitly by the categories as belonging together could equally well, from some other point of view, not belong to the same category. "Native American," asserted in usage as denoting a single grouping, comprises over 540 distinctive groups, among them 119 federally recognized tribes, each with its own set of practices. "Asian and Pacific Islander" covers such a wide territory that it includes people who look nothing like each other, speak unrelated languages, and have different histories. Similarly, "Hispanic," "white," and "black" each brought together a variety of groups who, from other viewpoints, did not share category traits. Analysis needs to uncover the point of view from which the category set is being constructed. It is this point of view that makes the particular assignment of elements to different categories, and the construction of the set of categories themselves, make sense.

Note, in this case, that the initial set of subcategories for Question 4—white, black, American Indian, Asian or Pacific Islander—is not in alphabetical order, one of the forms often used to indicate equivalence among categories. Chronological ordering is another such form, but it does not hold here either: "Hispanics" settled the Rio Grande valley before Jamestown, and "whites" encountered American Indians before they encountered "blacks." Here, it is the significance of the encounter that is being implicitly noted. To my way of thinking, this suggests that the categories reflect the point of view of a creator, on the Eastern seaboard or as far west as Chicago, of a particular European heritage for whom the encounter with African Americans was (before and during the Civil War) and still is (through the Civil Rights movements and subsequent debates over affirmative action) more significant than his encounter with Indians, Asians, or Hispanics.

Category analysis, then, helps identify the architecture of the argument that underlies a policy issue and that, while often not discussed explicitly in policy debates, nevertheless is part of policy-relevant publics' sense-making. These meanings are carried in the tacit knowledge shared within and among interpretive communities, which is embodied in the category structures. One way to read the history of homelessness in Massachusetts (Schon and Rein, 1994, chap. 6), for example, is in the shifting meanings of the category names that appear in policy debate over time, from skid row alcoholics and transients to the deinstitutionalized mentally ill, from evicted working class families to hoboes, from the unemployed to battered women. Other policy issues may not present such a wide-ranging categorizing structure, but category analysis is useful nonetheless. Gusfield (1976) shows how the policy category of the "drinking driver" implies a "nondrinking driver," with attendant implications for policy action. The classification scheme can itself be the subject of policy debate, but even when it is not, knowing what the category labels mean, who they include and exclude, and how the lines are drawn can figure centrally in the crafting and enacting of policies. The abortion issue revolves around only two categories: in their own words, "pro-choice" and "pro-life." These labels themselves make part of the argument: category analysis shows that the more conceptually accurate pairings would be pro-choice and anti-choice, or pro-life and anti-life. In the same way, that is, that "race" or "Asian American" makes a conceptual argument, so, too, do these two labels. Further analysis of position papers, speeches, placards, and other sources of language, as reported in the media, reveals that the two categories entail a set of positions on a number of dimensions, ranging from medical to religious to governmental. Looking for the organizing principles—"What are the elements of these two categories? The same and different with respect to what?"—brings these dimensions to light. They are identified in Table 3.3.

This analytic approach is similar to the more general, non-category-oriented frame analysis used by Linder (1995), Pal (1995), and Rein and Schon (1977), as well as to anthropologists' and linguists' approaches to category analysis (see Chapter 2 of this volume, and Lakoff, 1987).[11]

Table 3.3 An Architecture of Abortion Categories and Their Dimensions

	"Pro-choice"	*"Pro-life"*
Dimensions		
Individual rights	*Right* to choose → woman	*Right* to choose → fetus
(Legal-constitutional frame)		(Fetus needs representative = advocate)
(Fetus as property?)		(Define legal standing ["personhood"] of fetus)
Decision-making capability (choice as "decision")	Right to *choose* → woman	Right to *choose* → father/husband or parent of minor
(Woman as property?)	(Invoke state support of woman's right)	(Fetus needs representative = state/church)
Religion (Is fetus a living entity?, "ensoulment," quickening)	Separation of church and state; or nondenominational, universal	Church (fundamental Protestant or Catholic)
Moral	Individual conscience	Murder (defined by church, state)
Medical/technological (physical health)	Reproductive health; injury, death	[Mental health link]*
Mental health	Injured by bearing	Injured by aborting
Institutional	No child care, no money	Adopt it out (provide child for childless)

* This could be a logical counterargument, but has not been developed.

Narrative Analysis

What has been called "the interpretive turn" in social science (see, e.g., Rabinow and Sullivan, 1979) refocused theory and research on questions of meaning, as noted previously. More recently, this concern with meaning has led to a renewed attention to the role of stories or narratives as conveyors of meaning. Applications of narrative theory have developed in several fields, among them psychology, nursing, history, and education. Story and narrative elements have also shown up in methodological concerns: in seeking to articulate the "goodness" of an interpretation, theorists have identified criteria similar to the requirements for a good story—internal consistency, a logical flow (having a clear beginning, middle, and end), and other elements (e.g., the wealth of detail) that persuade the reader or listener that the interpreter knows intimately what happened, has an insider's understanding and a plausible explanation. Narrative analysis has also been applied to academic theorizing, though largely in fields other than public policy. Attention is paid to the rhetorical devices used to persuade readers of the validity and/or veracity of the writing, according to the canons of the discipline.[12] Literature (of the "belles lettres" variety) has also been read for its storytelling power and insight into policy and agency life: George Orwell's *Shooting an Elephant* for lessons in authority and Joseph Heller's *Catch 22* or *Something Happened* (especially chap. 1) for lessons in bureaucratic relationships and human emotion, are two examples (see Czarniawska-Joerges & Guillet de Monthoux, 1994; Waldo, 1968). Narrative approaches in policy analysis are relatively new, and my purpose here is to provide an overview of these developments and refer the reader to some key sources, rather than to illustrate their use.

From the perspective of narrative in general, analysts, policymakers, and other actors in policy, organizational, and community situations are seen as telling stories, whether for purposes of argument or claims-making (the analytic approach of political science) or for the expression of individual identity (a more psychological approach). In organizational, policy, and other acts, narratives both create meaning and give it shape: narrative is a "form of human comprehension that is productive of meaning by its imposition of a certain formal coherence on a virtual chaos of events" (White, 1981, p. 251). Narratives relate things that are understood to have happened; they are fashioned out of all sorts of experiences. In their telling—their engagement and enactment—they also become, themselves, sources of meaning, even when their storied nature is neither explicit nor, at times, recognized. "Events don't tell themselves" (T. Todorov, Introduction to Poetics, as quoted in O'Connor, 1996, p. 39).[13]

Narrative analysis has been applied to various policy actors, including analysts, as well as to policies themselves. Although there is a strong movement in other fields to analyze actors' personal stories as ways in which they express and develop their identity (see, e.g., Riessman, 1993), this focus has been underplayed in policy analysis, due (I suspect) to its public, collective, action orientation. Rather, narrative policy analysis has focused on the issue-oriented stories told by policy actors, using such analysis to clarify policy positions and perhaps mediate among them. Work of this sort analyzes the structure either of the policy and agency stories told by various actors or of their content, allowing comparison across different versions. Treating "story narrative" as a metaphor, the policy analyst can be led to identify "protagonists" and "antagonists" in a policy actor's story about the issue, the metaphors that describe the relationships between them, and the anticipated or desired transformations in them or in the policy situation captured by the "plot's" conflict or tensions and resolutions (McCoy, 1995, chap. 2; see also Buker, 1987). The plot motif of desired change embodies the values, beliefs, and/or feelings of the narrator—what is meaningful to him—and a comparison of such narratives can elicit differences of meaning across actors and their interpretive communities.

Roe (1994) elaborates on a structural analysis, identifying in several case examples the narrative and counter-narrative constructed by contending parties to policy controversies. He shows how case events could be retold from a different point of view, thereby constructing a "meta-narrative" such that the seemingly intractable controversies were no longer the focus and the parties were enabled to engage in discussion and move toward resolution. As he notes, "Sometimes what we are left to deal with are not the facts—that is why there is a controversy—but the different stories people tell as a way of articulating and making sense of the uncertainties and complexities that matter to them" (p. ix). Schon and Rein (1994), using the terminology of "frames" and "reframing," appear to follow a roughly similar method, showing how the metaphoric aspects of language in particular create a way of thinking about and acting on a policy issue (although their notion of reframing is not as formal a method as Roe's meta-narrative, which he borrows from the work of literary theorist Michael Riffaterre; see especially chap. 7).

Maynard-Moody (1993) also uses a structural analysis of policy actors' stories, but he focuses more on mapping the architecture of their content— the logical relations between events as narrated in different actors' stories— and comparing their similarities and differences. What interested him was how public managers make sense of their relationships with elected officials. In both Roe's and Maynard-Moody's approaches, the asymmetries (Roe's term) in narrative structure and content signal to the analyst the presence of deep-rooted uncertainties or power differentials, which may not otherwise be apparent. Power differentials, as Roe notes (1994, p. 72), work themselves out as people change their stories. The role of the policy analyst using these methods is to enable people to articulate their stories: "differential access [to information used in decision making] itself must become the focus of intervention and rectification" (p. 73). Abma (1997) and van Eeten (1997) also link their analyses to action, the one showing how vocational rehabilitation therapists' stories facilitate change, the other, how actors' stories about flooding and dike improvement led to policy action. Both point to issues surrounding stories not uttered or not heard.

Narrative research has also explored the ways in which policy analysts' analyses themselves shape debate on policy issues. As Fischer and Forester (1993, p. 2) note, policy analysis is itself an argumentative narrative practice—a practice that uses rhetoric to persuade to a point of view—and the chapters in their book provide case examples of such shaping. In some of the cases (the chapter by Throgmorton in particular), the line between policy actors and policy analysts blurs; or, to put the point differently, from an ethnomethodological point of view, those attending a meeting of the Mayor's Energy Task Force reviewing the Edison contract (Throgmorton, 1993) *were* policy analysts: community and consumer group representatives, task force members, and observers were in fact acting out the role of policy analysts, making sense of the discussion and formulating their own analyses of it.[14] Wagenaar (1997) argues that policy analysts narrate their daily work, that the structure of policy analytic practice parallels the structure of stories, and that these stories offer practitioners guides for action.

A more psychological orientation of life history narratives (Linde, 1993; Riessman, 1993) is found in analyses of clients' experiences as a way of understanding the effect of policies through implementation processes. Several essays in Abma (in press) explore this in the context of program evaluation. In a very different vein, some analysts have shifted focus from the stories told by individual actors to a consideration of public policies themselves as collective stories narrated by polities (state, local, federal) through legislation and implementation. The purpose of such narration parallels that of individuals: the polity tells an identity story through its drafting, discussing, passing, and enacting of a policy. So, for example, several authors in Schram and Neisser (1997) argue that various U.S. domestic and foreign policies express origin, group, and national identity stories, an argument I have also made with respect to U.S. race-ethnic policies (Yanow, in press). My favorite example is that of the nuclear-free zone policies adopted by several cities in the United States (see Chapter 6 in this volume). It could also be useful to see agency buildings, with their vocabularies of design elements and building materials, as telling policy stories (Yanow, 1995b; space analysis is treated at length in the next chapter).

In none of these approaches does the analyst focus on the "truth value" of the stories told, nor does the analyst seek to establish the primacy of one story version over all others. What these various approaches have in common is an appreciation that policy meaning is indeterminate and that there are multiple "readers" as well as "readings" of policy and agency "texts." The language of narrative or story or frame enables a focus on the active engagement of clients, community members, and others outside decision-making contexts in making sense of the policy world. The metaphors of narrative and story encourage us to ask about authors and storytellers, readers and hearers, plots and story lines, settings, and characters, and to see how authors, readers, and settings may also be characters in their own stories. "Narrative" focuses on structures and sequences: what meanings, made by whom, with what congruences and conflicts among them? "Story" focuses on plot and on the acts of telling and hearing—on intentions and attentions—helping policy analysts explore relationships between language and action. In listening to these narratives, the policy analyst is likely to encounter metaphors, categories, markings, and other sense-making elements that reflect and shape local knowledge and help analyze that knowledge. Although a narrative method for policy analysis has not yet been fully worked out, these various treatments suggest fruitful lines for further development.

NOTES

1. The following section is based on Yanow (1996b), chap. 5. Much attention has been given to the epistemological role of metaphors in theorizing (e.g., Brown, 1976; McCloskey, 1985; Morgan, 1986). My focus here, however, is on their role in policy language and practice.

2. Much of this debate is captured in Black (1962) and Ortony (1979).

3. Geertz (1973, p. 93) notes that cultural patterns have the dual aspect of giving meaning to "reality" by shaping themselves to that reality—being models *of* it—as well as by shaping that reality to themselves—being models *for* it.

4. For a related, albeit different, analytic approach, see Feldman's (1994, pp. 22-30) discussion of semiotic clustering.

5. This is described in more detail in Yanow (1996b), 142-146.

6. The following section is based on Yanow (1996a, 1998a, 1998b).

7. See Lakoff (1987, pp. 59-60) on marking and on categorizing from a linguistic approach. For other approaches to category analysis similar to the one outlined here, see Douglas (1966, 1975, 1982) and Edelman (1977, 1995).

8. These are the only questions that have direct bearing on racial and ethnic population features. Questions about religion are not included in the census, following the principle of separation of church and state. The language question is germane because language is commonly considered a component of ethnicity.

9. In fact, as Ralph Brower notes (personal correspondence, 1997), "Eskimo" itself is a term borrowed from Algonquin Indians, the "Eskimos'" neighbors to the south in Canada. It is Algonquin for "eater of raw flesh" (an apparent reference to the practice of eating raw, usually frozen, fish). Those referred to in this fashion identify themselves as Inupiaq and Yupik, two groups that are distinct in their language, geographic location, subsistence, and other cultural patterns (Brower notes that the Yupiks do not eat raw fish,

as far as he knows). Yet census practices meld the two groups into one, under an imposed name.

10. An exception to this could be when there is a contesting metaphor in policy debate, which would make the contrasting case explicit; e.g., urban blight vs. gentrification; homelessness vs. deinstitutionalization.

11. I thank John Van Maanen for helping me clarify this link. Lakoff (1996) attempted to bring this mode of linguistic analysis to the domain of politics and policy issues, but both his data sources and methods of analysis are unclear.

12. See, for example, McCloskey (1985) in economics; in organizational studies, Golden-Biddle and Locke (1993), Hatch (1996), and Smircich (1995); in anthropology, Clifford (1988), Geertz (1988), Marcus and Fischer (1986), and Van Maanen (1986); and in social theory more broadly, Brown (1976) and Tierney and Lincoln (1997). An excellent piece of such writing in policy analysis is Gusfield (1976); see also his lengthier treatment (1981). Czarniawska-Joerges (1992, 1993) treats events in public management—budgeting, organizational change—from narrative perspectives, but what she learns from these seems to be oriented more toward theory development than to practice-oriented analysis.

13. I thank Murray Edelman for bringing out these points. The literature on narrative theory is vast. O'Connor (1996) presents an extensive overview; see also Polkinghorne (1988).

14. This point was brought home to me by Paris and Reynolds' (1983, chap. 6) discussion of applications of ethnomethodology to policy analysis. See also Kaplan (1986) on policy analyses as stories and Throgmorton (1991) on policy analysis as rhetoric. Hood and Jackson (1994) extend this line of argument to public administration.

4. SYMBOLIC OBJECTS

Policy meanings are communicated and interpreted not just through policy and implementing agency language, but also through objects—physical artifacts—initiated or modified by policy language and/or by agencies as they enact that language.

Symbolic objects typically figure in conveying policy meanings in two forms: built spaces and policy programs. The first of these includes the settings of policy enactment and their decor or "props."[1] Policies create agencies or agency departments to enact the programs named in policy language, and this often entails creating or modifying spaces or places for them. These settings of policy and agency acts may communicate policy meanings other than, in addition to, or even contradicting those named in the policies themselves. Second, policy language creates programs, such as housing allowance programs, national health insurance, or welfare support, and the objects entailed in these programs—a house or good health or food stamps—may represent meanings other than those explicitly named in and denoted by policy language.

Certainly, programs entail language use, and space use entails acts, but for analytic purposes it can be useful to isolate a focus on objects and explore their contribution to the communication of meaning.

Built Spaces and Their "Props"

The spaces designed, built, or modified for implementing agencies or for policy programs may communicate policy meanings. For example, although many would say that the purpose of schools is to teach course substance, an analysis of space use shows that they also teach obedience to authority: in traditional classroom design, students sit in rows and lines of squared off desks that allow them to face in only one direction, constraining movement and focusing interactions with teachers in formal exchanges (which is reinforced behaviorally when the standing teacher leans over them as they bend to do their work; it was against this constrained, authority-oriented space-body arrangement that "open classrooms" and discussion circles were created as new educational policies). To draw another example, 19th-century New England factories, as well as schools, were built to resemble churches, thereby bringing church behavior—quiet, order, and deference to authority—into their settings (M. R. Smith, MIT Lectures on Technology in America, as cited in Sclove, 1989). And the design of social service waiting rooms, which requires clients to form lines, enacts their restricted agency and their submission to others' directives.

Analysis of built spaces (including, when appropriate, their decor, furnishings, or "props") can focus on one or both of the ways in which spaces communicate meanings: through their use and through their materials. Built spaces act on their users—through such design elements as their mass, interior proportions and shape, and use of light—to evoke feeling, in the emotive, aesthetic, and kinesthetic senses of that word, and associated behavioral responses. Their communicative power is felt, then, not only through aesthetic appreciation at a distance but even more strongly in their use, through the arousal of emotional and physical responses.[2] Museum buildings of traditional design, for example, lead the visitor to look upwards—up the long, broad, imposing staircase—prior to entry.[3] The physical feeling this causes—standing with the head tilted back, at times at a severe angle—places the museum building and, by extension, its contents, at a physical and psychological-emotional remove, "on a pedestal," emphasizing the "don't touch me" sacredness of the exhibited objects (which is, in traditional museums, underscored by exhibit policies and display design). By contrast, the main entrance of California's Oakland Museum steps down to a plaza, intentionally enacting its founders' desire to make the museum accessible, creating the opposite feeling from the veneration instilled by more traditional museum buildings, even before the visitor has entered the exhibit space (Yanow, 1998c). Police departments, courts, military bases, welfare offices, universities, and other public and nonprofit agencies implementing public policies similarly use spatial design, the physical experience it engenders, and the feelings it evokes to communicate desired behavioral responses, and these may either support or contradict policy meanings.

Interpretive analysis of built space draws on the researcher-analyst's participative experiences as proxy for others' behaviors and actions: Through those firsthand, immediate experiences the analyst gains entree into understanding others' responses. It might be helpful to think of space as a kind of nonverbal language, with a vocabulary and rhetoric of its own. To interpret written or oral language (such as in analyzing documents or interviews), the researcher-analyst must share an understanding (with the writer or speaker) of its grammar. He uses his own understanding of language, of its rules, its structure, its words, to grasp the other's meaning. To understand nonverbal communication (such as gestures, posture, dress, motion), the researcher-analyst also draws on prior knowledge of its grammar and meaning. Similarly with space and its communicative modes, the researcher-analyst understands what is being "said" through his own bodily experience of the space and his associated affective and behavioral responses. These become surrogates for others' responses, much in the same way that his own understanding of language use helps him comprehend others' speech or writing. The researcher-analyst relies on his familiarity with, if not membership in, the culture of those designing and/or using the space (or speaking or writing), its practices and modes of communication, and the meanings connoted by these various vocabularies, grammars, and rhetorics. If "the self is the instrument of research" in field-based methods more broadly, as Van Maanen (1996) notes with respect to ethnography, it is all the more so in the analysis of space. This use of the analyst's own kinesthetic, affective, and behavioral experience as proxy for that of others, in an initial effort to understand the values, beliefs, and feelings inculcated by the built spaces, underscores the provisional quality of the analyst's interpretations. These provisional inferences must be followed up with other observation, interviews, and/or document analysis to corroborate or refute them.

Two examples of the emotive quality of space suggest the general character of this kind of analysis and the role of personal response in it. Although neither is directly policy-related, I include them because they are more vivid examples of the role of space in affecting feeling and behavior than those usually encountered in the realm of public policy, and so are useful to demonstrate the general point. Whereas examples from the policy world are typically less dramatic, space nonetheless may affect users' assessments of policy or program intent.

In an analysis of the American Immigrant Museum of Honor at Ellis Island, I discovered to my surprise on entering the building that it was not clear where to go.[4] The room was immense, its ceiling the height of the third floor, its breadth seemingly longer than a football field, with a staircase at either end. In the middle of the floor were two desks, and I headed toward them. That seemed to be the logical starting point, since it was not clear which of the two staircases led to the beginning of the exhibit. But after a few steps it became apparent that I would find no clearer information there than I already had. I saw no posted signs, no arrows on the floor to indicate direction, and the spatial vocabulary gave no signal, other than the two staircases. I was almost immobilized: would I go the wrong way, start the exhibit from the end, miss a crucial part? How would I find out what the special exhibits were and whether I wanted to see them?

I became irritated that the visual cues for movement—in an agency intended to serve the public—were not clearer. My annoyance activated me. I arbitrarily picked one of the staircases, climbed up, and entered the fascinating world of photographs, artifacts, recorded voices, and texts that led from one room to another (and, as it turned out, moved through much of the exhibit from end to beginning). About two hours later, halfway down one of the staircases looking over the massive entrance hall, I started, recalling my earlier confusion: I must have recapitulated the experience of confusion felt by immigrants entering the space between 40 and 110 years earlier! Theirs would have been magnified, of course, not only not knowing where to go, but whether they would be allowed to stay and what would befall them. What brilliance on the part of the museum designers, I thought—or serendipity (and I have not yet been able to ascertain which). This experience of the space and its "feel" and meaning provided me with an inference about designers' intentions and visitors' responses. Such an analysis might have been part of an evaluation of the National Park Service's compliance with the Americans with Disabilities Act or an assessment of service provision more generally, as part of an anticipated policy revision. Had I been taking the research further, I would have sought to corroborate or refute these provisional hypotheses through observation of other visitors' actions and conversational interviews with them and with the museum designers and founders.

In another analysis, of the United States Holocaust Memorial Museum soon after its opening, ropes guiding passage toward a guard standing in front of an elevator door signaled the entrance to the display area. I knew that in contemporary museum design, it has become customary "to elevator" visitors to the top floor and let them work their way down. Assuming these to be procedural cues, I followed the ropes to the opening, showed my ticket with its time stamp, and walked toward the elevator. I entered with about five others. It was a large elevator; we were not crowded. The doors closed. The elevator did not move.

I did not like being enclosed and immobilized. I had a destination, and the elevator was not taking me there. I became aware that it was dimly lit. I could barely make out the details of the faces shut in with me. I looked up to see if a bulb had burned out—in such a new museum!—and discovered that there was only a single, low wattage, bare bulb in the ceiling. I then discovered one of the reasons it was so dark inside: the walls of the elevator were painted a steel gray, as was the floor. They were bare walls, without the paneling commonly found in modern elevators. There was no decoration. But neither was it a typical freight elevator. I was beginning to search for the control panel and an "open door" button when the elevator began its slow ascent. I assumed we would soon arrive on the top floor. I was eager to get out and get on with my viewing.

It stopped. The doors opened. Light, air—confusion. There was a large, open space immediately outside the elevator doors, filled with people milling about, some trying to get into a room where a video was being screened, others trying to move down a corridor that immediately narrowed as it led by the exhibits. The exhibits were displayed in clusters behind floor-to-ceiling glass, in chronological order. I tried to pass behind the crowd and get a view over their heads of the displays. Movement was impossible. I began to feel stuck again, like in the unmoving elevator, barred from fresh air and light.

This time, reflection on what I was experiencing came almost immediately. The elevator had simulated a railroad boxcar used by the Third Reich, I thought, although without crowding, or perhaps a concentration camp "shower" room. The corridor had similarly (re)created the physical experience of crowding, with movement possible in only one direction. Although I suspected that the design-invoked experience was intentional on the part of the architects—there had been enough critical coverage of the museum in the newspapers to suggest this, as well as interviews that made it explicit—newspaper reportage suggested that not all of it was. Although the design intentionally controls movement along a prescribed path, the numbers of visitors were unanticipated and overwhelming, creating unintended bottlenecks. Subsequent document analysis and others' reported interviews corroborated that my experience was, in fact, both intended by building designers and experienced by other visitors. Once again, this could have been part of an evaluation assessing the implementation of a policy whose programs depended for their success on the use of specially designed spaces.

Less dramatic, but nonetheless critical, examples come from city and county government departments whose mission statements explicitly name a welcoming, service-oriented policy, yet whose physical spaces and props send contradictory messages.

These examples illustrate how space use can communicate meaning. Building materials may also communicate policy meanings. Interpretive policy analysis of building design and materials proceeds by contrast and comparison, either to a local context or to a class of building or agency not tied to a particular locale (depending on the policy and agency being analyzed). For example, analysis of the Oakland Museum building puts it in the context of what is often called "the museum world," as its design elements contrast explicitly with more traditional museum building design. The Israel Corporation of Community Centers (ICCC) analysis, on the other hand, compares the center buildings to other local public agency buildings and to local residences (see Table 4.1), as they were intended by their founders and creators to stand in contrast with local spaces and activities (as seen, for instance, in a quote in the next section).

As I read agency documents, I noticed that much attention was paid to community center design. Visiting centers around the country produced an odd experience: no matter which town I entered, I could pick out the ICCC center without asking, just by attending to its design elements, including building materials. One early agency document led me to focus analysis on the contrast with surrounding buildings. It read, in part, that the community center should present to the local residents "a pleasant atmosphere of social and cultural well-being which is often absent from their impoverished dwellings" (Israel Corporation of Community Centers, 1971). I saw that the design, scale, and mass of the community centers stood them in marked contrast to other nearby public agency buildings, as well as to local residential buildings. They took up space not only in terms of their large scale but also in terms of their set-offs from adjacent buildings. Space use combined with the costliness and quality of building materials (wood, glass) and furnishings (radios and television sets at a time when these were prohibitively expensive for local families to purchase, plus tennis courts and swimming pools) set the community centers apart not just in physical terms but in

Table 4.1 Siting, Materials, and Decor: Analysis by Contrast

Community Center	Residence	Other Public Buildings
Siting/Scale/Design		
central location	radiate from center	central and dispersed
broad entrance plaza	small approach	small or no approach
wide entrance doors	in scale	small and in scale
massive, oversized scale	in scale	in scale
set apart on four sides	close proximity	adjoining; or small yard
oversized entry rooms, halls	small rooms	small interiors
renowned architectural design	no	no
American concept	no	no
Materials		
stone facade, with glass	stucco	stucco
wood paneling	—	—
Decor		
"European"-style furnishings	less costly	plain furnishings
radio, TV	not affordable	not affordable or appropriate to job
"oil" paintings (reproductions)	no	no
tennis court, swimming pool	no	no

SOURCE: Yanow 1996b, page 173.

material terms as well. The command of resources and the power and status represented by these various objects communicated a class-based, Western "otherness." Document analysis substantiates that this was the intent of agency founders. Policymakers, agency executives, and founders intended the center buildings to provide local children with "escape" from what the planners saw as their overcrowded homes. As one observer noted, "The centers that have lots of activities are those which are built very differently from the way the community's houses are built. The more closely the community center resembles the houses, I would predict that it would be less successful" (interview, 1979).

In observing agency buildings and spaces and studying spatial contrasts, the analyst potentially attends to several design elements (again, depending on the specific study) and their meanings in the specific context (both time and place). These may include one or more of the following:

- size, scale, mass—which may symbolize costliness, quality, power (to physically take up space is, in many cultures, a sign of power and control);[5]
- materials—which also symbolize costliness and quality;

- the historical or aesthetic reference points of architectural design (e.g., Greek columns, modern styling)—which may represent certain values, beliefs or feelings;
- siting (location) and proximity to or distance from surrounding spaces and/or buildings—which may represent power (the command of space), resources, or both;[6]
- landscaping, in terms of both the materials (costliness, quality, well kept or not) and the use of space (commanding or not);
- decor, furnishings, or "props" (including signage), which may, through intrinsic value, represent costliness or quality, and whose reference points (e.g., so-called "Scandinavian" furniture) may also carry meaning.[7]

Other design elements may not have a policy-specific symbolic component—the use of light and dark, for example—but these may nonetheless affect users' emotional and behavioral responses to the spaces and be carried over to policy-related interpretations.

Before ascribing intentionality to policy and building designers in evoking the responses to built spaces that users experience, it is important to know whether a building or space was designed for the agency using it in implementing policy or whether the space was designed for some other purpose and taken over by that agency. Many people are not consciously aware of the power of built space to communicate meaning, and policymakers and agency administrators are often unaware of the effect their spaces have on clients and other policy-relevant publics. An analyst attuned to these processes can do much to bring an awareness of spatial communication and interpretation to bear on space-using policies' implications and effects.

Programs

The other main subcategory of objects that communicate meaning in a policy context is that of programs. Housing policies, for example, have entailed the use of vouchers, direct payments to landlords, or incentives to developers to encourage the provision of low-income housing. Both policies and programs have depended, at least in part, on the meaning of "house" or home ownership in contemporary American society: shelter or status, security or investment. A program that offers the means to acquire housing through subsidized purchase embodies the range of cultural meanings symbolized by "home" and ownership. Policy proposals for gun control programs depend on the meaning of "gun possession"; a gun in this context "is not simply an instrument, but a symbol imbued with meanings about individual autonomy, social risk, the frontier," and so on (Pal, 1996). The specific meanings of policy programs may often vary across interpretive communities. Activities and internal programs created by agencies in the process of implementing public policy programs also figure in this way. The initial steps in analyzing programs follow the general format identified earlier in Table 1.1: ascertain whether there is a program-related object at the heart of the policy in question that has symbolic meaning for potential clients, legislators, implementors, and other policy-relevant publics; determine what it means to members of different interpretive communities; assess whether these meanings are complementary or conflicting. If different policy-relevant communities interpret the object differently, problems are likely to arise in the implementation of the policy.

In the ICCC case, the ways in which some of the programs figured centrally in communicating policy meanings were not readily apparent. A partial list of programs offered at centers in the agency's early years includes karate, judo, wrestling, weight lifting, folk dance, ballet, jewelry making, batik, photography, sewing, recorder lessons, guitar, painting, homework help, English, Hebrew, Arabic, French, bible study, "parenting," and Citizens' Information. While participating in one center and observing at others, I came to see that ballet classes were significant in a way that others were not. What led me to this understanding was the observation that ballet classes were always oversubscribed, while others were not, and full of a charged energy and attention that was not present around other activities, children's or adults'. This was manifest, among other things, in the level of adult participation and excitement surrounding the classes. Furthermore, the director, secretary, and librarian of one center paid what seemed to me to be extraordinary attention to enrollments in and management of this one area of programming. In reading agency memos, correspondence, annual reports, and other materials, I discovered that this special attention was not unique to the dancing children, their siblings and parents, and center staff: ballet classes were also meaningful to agency founders and administrators. That this was the case, and what the intended meaning of "ballet" in this agency and policy context was, became clear from the following excerpt from a letter written by one of the founders:

> How proud some of the citizens [of this development town] must now feel that even their youngsters can study ballet. . . . It is not ballet that is important, but the fact that . . . the youngsters of the poor have an equal opportunity to be exposed to today's cultural activities as are the youngsters of the [major city] residents. (correspondence, 9/29/72)

Conversational interviews with center clients revealed that many of them also shared this view of the meaning of "ballet" and its availability in the community centers. One woman who enrolled her two daughters in her community center's ballet classes commented that the cost put such classes out of reach of many of her friends and neighbors, but she was thankful that the class gave her girls a chance to acquire "what urban children had." Other conversations supported the concept that center programs figured symbolically in helping local residents feel they were bridging a gap between themselves and city residents. One high school Youth Council organized by a community center was discussing a program that entailed hosting a Youth Council from a major nearby city. While the teenagers were highly sensitized to perceived differences and their own inadequacies—one of the teenagers remarked: "They're so much better than we are. How can we possibly host them?"—their adult advisers argued that their center programs put them on an equal footing. Further analysis linked this set of meanings to policy purposes.

Program and activity meanings are not necessarily static, and often change as general societal values change or in response to other influences. Because of this, the meaning(s) of programs must be interpreted in the time and place contexts in which they were created and used. For example, in 1973 one rural community center offered tennis lessons among their other sports classes, but only one high school junior signed up. Tennis was seen at the time as an elite, "Anglo" sport; it had no audience within Israel and no local appeal. Between 1975 and 1978 a professional tennis trainer started coaching youngsters at the Tel Aviv Country Club, entering them successfully in international competitions. News coverage reported the prize moneys, and a national tennis court and stadium were built outside Tel Aviv. By 1980 the same rural community center had more requests for tennis classes than it could handle. Policy meanings, in other words, were not initially communicated through tennis programs; these acquired symbolic significance as they came to represent the Western, urban values that center programs and policies were intended to inculcate.

Abstracted from the extended analysis, these examples of ballet and tennis would seem to be far removed from the world of policy analysis and relevant, if at all, only to the world of meaning internal to the agency and its clients and staff. However, policy meanings are often communicated and interpreted in such details as the activities, programs, and built spaces in and through which the policy is carried out or projected to be carried out. When object analysis is brought together with language and/or act analysis, the themes that emerge in one—the policy meanings suggested,

Table 4.2 Parallel Connotations of Language and Object Symbols

	Supermarket metaphor	*Connotation*	*Community center design*
Size	big	modern, exciting, fashionable → "American"	spacious
Location	central, cities	modern, upscale	central to town or neighborhood
Quality of Goods	endless variety, standardized	upscale	many programs, "pre-packaged" (not local; made in headquarters)
Source of Competition	*shuk, makolet,* limited supply	small, crowded, old-fashioned, peripheral, parochial (by contrast with community center)	youth club, old, rundown movie theater or assembly hall

for example, in an agency's use of built space—are often discovered to be complemented by those found in another. This is illustrated in the context of the foregoing metaphor and space analysis of the ICCC case, in Table 4.2, which shows how both the supermarket metaphor and the community center building design and materials connoted parallel meanings. Further analysis of other elements showed how these meanings influenced the agency's implementation of its policy mandate.

Summary

In general, analysis of built space and policy programs may begin with:

1. observation, including listening to policy actors talk about the policy and observing space use and program-related activities;
2. document analysis, to see if policy actors write about particular objects as significant carriers of meaning (to them).

These initial assessments may be corroborated or refuted by subsequent interviews (formal, informal, or both). The range of meanings will depend on the context (issue, time, place, people and groups involved). Comparative analysis (of agency buildings with other sorts of buildings, of one program with another, depending on the context) can be helpful in gaining insight into these meanings.

NOTES

1. Burke (1969), in his dramaturgical analysis, identified the scene or the setting as one of five analytic elements (the others being the agent, the act, agency [the means of acting], and purpose). This approach was taken up later by Edelman (1964). See Feldman (1994) for a summary of Burke's analytic method.
2. Lakoff and Johnson (1980) note the extent to which interrelated spatial and bodily experiences permeate American English. Discussing common orientational metaphors—up-down, front-back, central-peripheral, and so forth—and their associated meanings—"up" is associated with control, for example: "He's at the *height* of his power" (p. 15)—they write: "These spatial orientations arise from the fact that we have bodies of the sort we have and that they function as they do in our physical environment" (p. 14). On the social meanings of public spaces, see also Edelman (1995), Lasswell (1979), the essays in Goodsell (1993), and the extensive overview of this field in Goodsell (1988, chap. 1).
3. Museum exhibits have been the subject of extensive analysis (see, e.g., Karp and Lavine, 1991), their buildings less so. See Clifford's essay in that collection for one example.
4. This and the next example are based on Yanow, 1998c.
5. In many cultures height and broad shoulders in a man are signs of physical power and financial or social stature, another reflection of space use recapitulating bodily experience.
6. Analyses of gender and class relations in the workplace, as well as of human posture in general, make related points. Many women, and men feeling depressed or powerless, tend to sit and carry themselves with rounded shoulders and dropped head—hence, being "in a slump." Confident, powerful people expand their shoulders and chests and use their arms to take up more space—in the extreme, we speak of such a person as a "stuffed shirt" or "full of him- or herself." It is those in power—typically, man to woman, superiors to subordinates—who touch their opposites but are not touched by them in return, like the building that is set apart from its neighbors. See, for example, the analyses in Hearn et al. (1990).
7. There is a wide range of objects used within organizations to communicate meaning that could also be analyzed under the heading of objects. These would include, for example, the use of plants, sculpture, artwork, and other decorative items; the display of personal artifacts such as family pictures and diplomas; awards, trophies, and other symbols of achievement; and so on. These, however, usually represent meanings that are agency- or industry-specific, rather than linking to a policy issue being implemented by the agency in question, although that is not impossible. For analyses of such objects, see, e.g., the essays in Gagliardi (1990) and Kunda (1992).

5. SYMBOLIC ACTS

Policy-relevant groups interpret a wide range of acts, from agenda-setting acts to acts of legislating and implementing, as communicating policy meanings. Often, the mere act of agreeing to hold hearings on a policy issue is intended to be, and is, understood by policy-relevant publics. It conveys, for example, a validation of the importance of the issue in the eyes of "the public" as well as in the eyes of "the government" that has allocated resources (time, money, personnel) to the hearings. The message that is often received is, "Your claim is being heard." Meanings are also communicated through the implementing acts of agencies enacting legislated policies. Anything the agency undertakes to do that (re)presents the policy to members of the public may be understood to communicate policy meanings. This is particularly so with the acts of street-level bureaucrats (Lipsky, 1979): as the agency actors with whom the public most frequently interacts, their actions are understood as conveying intended policy meanings.

Members of the public interpret other acts as well. Whereas agency administrators value the actual delivery of services (the outputs of an implementing organization), this is not the only act in which the "consumers" of those services may find meaning, as Colebatch (1995) notes. He cites the case of a veterans' agency that created a regional office. For agency administrators it was meaningful as a channel for the supply of services. Yet it was also read by others as a "symbolic affirmation of the esteem in which veterans are held" (p. 160); it provided veterans' association officeholders an opportunity "to demonstrate to their members the usefulness of association membership" (p. 160); and it was the occasion for a number of other interpretations, all of which became more visible and more explicit knowledge when "a reforming official [sought] to close the regional office on the basis that the services could be delivered more cheaply through the central office" (p. 160).

Acts stand in a representational relationship to the meanings understood or intended to underlie them.[1] The "local knowledge" about a policy issue, which a policy analyst is seeking to access, often includes interpretations of these various acts, and these interpretations may be at odds with what policymakers (whether legislators or agency actors) intend to communicate. Colebatch (1995) illustrates this with an example of different interpretations of policy evaluation acts instituted by the central Australian government for local agencies to carry out. Although presented as a "natural" part of the policy cycle (involving merely the execution of an objective, technical instrument), these evaluations were understood differently by various interpretive communities. Introduced by efficiency-minded legislators as a control measure, the act embodied the power of central government, and that power to demand such evaluations signaled an extension of central government over dispersed and independent agencies. This meaning was far more significant, in Colebatch's analysis, than the substance of any evaluation. For agency administrators, by contrast, evaluations provided a way of justifying budgetary allocations. At the same time, for point-of-service-delivery personnel (like Lipsky's street-level bureaucrats), evaluations constituted an interference with "real" work. Such variant interpretations—variant with respect to policymakers' intentions—are likely to produce actions other than those intended and anticipated, affecting policy implementation. This is the sort of local knowledge an analyst would want to access.

Sapolsky (1972) provides a different example of agency acts used to convey budgetary messages. Polaris missile developers needed to convince Congress that they were successfully implementing their mission—key to the continued funding essential for implementation—even before they had a missile to show for their work. They did so not by showing a finished product, but through the symbolic act of spending the whole of their allocated budget—an act that was "read" by Congress in keeping with developers' intent and that brought additional appropriations. The missile system's managers also used formal management information systems (MIS) tools (such as PERT, a "computerized R&D planning, scheduling, and control technique" [Sapolsky, 1972, p. 117]), thereby projecting the image of a modern, rational, successful agency whose budget requests were therefore deemed justified. Ingersoll and Adams (1992), in their study of the Washington State Ferry System, also show how the state Department of Transportation used MIS and other accounting tools to communicate the image of modern, rational management, and how these acts were interpreted by "ferry people" as being at odds with their traditional marine- and family-based practices.

Hofmann's (1995) study of technology policy in Germany presents yet another example of varying interpretations of acts. The transfer of technology from university research centers to business firms, with the support of government funds, rested on the way members of each of these three sectors interpreted the acts of the other two. These interpretations, however, were quite different from the understandings members of each sector had about their own acts, premises, and abilities. Each interpretive community—

university, business, government—possessed different localized knowledge (what Hofmann calls an "implicit theory") of the nature of the relationship. In the discrepancy between explicit theory and local knowledge, technology transfer lagged, and attempts to remediate what were perceived to be the problems were failing because they were addressed to these misperceptions, in ignorance of local knowledge.

Analyzing acts can be the most difficult of the three analytic categories, because they are the least visible to an outsider and their meanings are the least easily accessible. Accessing and understanding acts commonly requires more time because it typically takes longer for an outsider to become an admitted participant in a community or agency's "active" life, whereas built spaces and other objects and language of various forms are more readily observable and their meanings accessible through observation and interviews. This makes participant-observation or ethnography—the longer term in-dwelling among organizational or community members that balances the estrangement of the analytic observer with the familiarity of the group member—the most useful approach to accessing local knowledge about acts.

How does the analyst identify which acts, of the myriad engaged in a policy arena, are symbolic and worth focusing on? Although the answers will be site- and context-specific, some general guidelines can be identified. First, the acts of legislating, of holding hearings, of inviting (potential) clients' views—and the omission of any of these—often carry great meaning (especially in their absence). Second, significant acts often emerge from comparative analysis, especially one focused on the potential contrast between act and word (see Chapter 1). Many agencies, for example, proclaim in written and oral statements (sometimes published in annual reports, sometimes displayed on walls in offices and public spaces throughout the building) their mission to serve the community in all its diversity; yet in observing the agency in action, the researcher-analyst may discover that operating hours preclude working residents from availing themselves of these services or that agencies have not prepared informational documents and forms in languages that facilitate service delivery. Museums, for one, often state that their mission is to serve the public, but, at least until recently, most museums were open during hours that made it difficult for many members of the public (e.g., working people on day shifts) to visit. The hours of operation were suitable for tourists, housewives, the wealthy, school children, and others not tied to customary working hours, thereby instituting (or maintaining) a class connection that links to other elements of the institutional history of museums.

An analysis of a regional environmental mediation center provides an example of studying the contrast between word and act and the importance of local knowledge in illuminating that contrast.[2] Agency policy defined success as the completed, signed settlement of a dispute. In quantifying their case load, this meant a very low success rate, in their own eyes. I was asked, as part of a four-person team, to evaluate their work. In interviews, members of their client agencies indicated that the mediation center had been highly successful, even in situations that had not progressed to a formal settlement: mediators had helped them clarify their positions and discover unseen options, improved community ties and interorganizational relations, facilitated good relations beyond the immediate dispute, taught skills for future use, and enabled clients to proceed on their own. Client agency members defined success in terms of these and other steps along the way toward a formal mediated settlement, even when mediation stopped far short of such a written settlement. Bringing this local knowledge back to the center allowed its members to reexamine the full range of their acts and the meanings of those acts for their clients, and to reevaluate their sense of what they were doing.

Two other, more specific, forms of analysis can also be useful in analyzing policy-related acts: ritual analysis and myth analysis.

Ritual Analysis

In seeking to identify acts that are significant conveyors of meaning to various audiences, it is often useful to search for regularly repeated patterns of activity, which we commonly call "rituals." Bernstein (1977), for example, defines ritual as a "pattern of acts, specific to a situation, which construct a framework of meaning over and beyond the specific situational meanings" (p. 54). This approach to ritual treats it "as a form of cultural communication that transmits the cognitive categories and dispositions that provide people with important aspects of their sense of reality" (Bell, 1997, p. 2). In this sense, rituals may be seen in an expressive or performative mode, giving voice to social tensions and conflicts while shaping their meanings.[3]

While researching the central operations of the Israel Corporation of Community Centers (ICCC) over an extended period of time, I attended several annual meetings and also read reports of them, including summaries of the main speeches, in annual reports and other agency documents, covering the first decade of operations.[4] I noted that the executive director regularly asked those attending the annual meetings, "What are our goals?" At the end of that period, the head of Research and Planning wrote that the agency's goals and operating principles were only then beginning the process of "crystallization." At some point, while reflecting on what I was learning about the agency, this practice struck me as odd. Did this mean that there was no clear understanding prior to 1980 of what the agency's goals were? The ICCC had behaved for over 10 years very much as though it did have clear goals: it hired staff, built buildings, raised funds, created and carried out programs, and established an identity and an image. Wouldn't any agency with a clear, widely published mission statement—the ICCC called theirs the "Ten Operating Principles"—have a well-developed sense of its goals long before its tenth year of operations? I began to wonder why it was necessary to ask the goals question at all, let alone repetitively, and why in such a public forum as the annual meeting. This puzzle emerged from comparing one set of observed acts (the meetings) with another (daily work practices). The patterned repetitiveness led me to identify the goal-questioning as a "ritual" act and to explore it to see if it made sense in terms of possible underlying meanings in addition to its "literal" situational meanings.

The first step, then, in ritual analysis in a policy context is the recognition of a pattern: the identification of a regularly repeated, situation-specific set of acts, often in a specialized space (one not used for "normal" acts) and/or at a special time. But how is the analyst to know that this regularly recurring set of acts has *symbolic* meaning? How is one to know, for example, that the regularly scheduled 10 a.m. Friday meeting of the XYZ Committee is a "ritual" for policy analytic purposes rather than "just" a meeting? For an anthropologist or social psychologist, patterned, regularly repeated acts may have symbolic meaning in themselves in a social or societal context (e.g., in terms of their role in expressions of group or individual identity). For the policy analyst, the key lies in the relationship between the act itself and policy or implementing agency purposes, as expressed in legislative language or official documents, or in interviews with policymakers or agency executives. If there is an anomaly—a discrepancy between what one would expect (based on officials' documents or words, or the researcher-analyst's practical experience and knowledge of the situation) and what one finds (in deeds)—the researcher-analyst might suspect that the recurrent act is "constructing a framework of meaning," in Bernstein's (1977) words, over and beyond its explicit, instrumental, or literal purpose. Such was the case with the ICCC: based on observing its extensive infrastructure and daily operations, the researcher might reasonably expect an agency to know its goals well after ten years, yet expectation and observation did not mesh. The analyst seeks to decipher what this meaning might be: analysis proceeds by trying to discern a context in which the parts of the anomaly taken together make some sense other than the presenting instrumentality. This next step in this analysis is presented in the next section.

Another clue is also suggestive of frameworks of meaning beyond the indexical. "Ritual" is a term of analysis, not a commonplace, everyday adjective. When one colleague is overheard saying to another on Friday morning, "It's almost ten o'clock. Are you coming to the ritual?" the use of the term indicates that the weekly meeting is no longer being seen as "just" a meeting. Naming the recurring act a "ritual" (outside of an analytic context) negates its indexical meaning, but at the same time this ironic expression points to an additional sense-making framework beyond the indexical, within which the act does have meaning (even if ironic or negative). By exploring the tensions or contradictions between intended and enacted meanings, the analyst can begin to assess whether the act is communicating some additional policy-relevant meaning (other than the indexical meaning that it appears to convey).

In the case of American race-ethnic policies and practices, for example, one might see a policy ritual in the regularized practice created in many agencies of asking for race-ethnic identification (e.g., in universities, workplaces, the census, hospitals, and police departments). It is the only facet of individual identity that we are requested to name so often, other than perhaps our names themselves. This ritual may be seen as a way of enacting conflicting notions of race-ethnic identity, as something that can be named only by the individual (clear in the case of the census) versus something that can be named by an outside party (the employer, in EEOC policy). The first treats identity in keeping with a view of it as something subjective: changing, multiple, internal, dependent on context.[5] The second treats it as objective: essentialist, fixed, physical, and visible—anyone can tell what you "are" by looking and naming you according to the categories available in public discourse at this moment. A policy analyst seeking to explore local knowledge about the census, the Office of Management and Budget, EEO/AA (Equal Employment Opportunity/Affirmative Action), and other race-ethnic-related policy and program practices would have to analyze the interpretations of their acts made by various policy-relevant communities of meaning and the accompanying sense-shaping of race-ethnicity; identifying some of these acts as rituals may aid in that analysis.

Myth Analysis

Rituals are often the more visible and accessible enactments of myths: they preserve and propagate the values, beliefs, and feelings embedded in those myths (Lakoff and Johnson, 1980), drawing on language, objects, or both to do so.[6] Because myths are often acted out in this way, I include their analysis in this section. These are not the myths of written or oral folklore. The importance of their creation and enactment leads me to treat these myths as symbolic acts, rather than as symbolic language.

From an anthropological rather than a literary approach, myths may be seen as explanations constructed in the face of puzzling parts of their organizational or policy contexts. We create myths as an act of mediating contradictions, such as those that arise when we are faced with accommodating in daily life the mandates of two (or more) irreconcilable values. Myths direct our attention away from such incommensurables, from the puzzling aspects of policy and agency realities, suspending them in a temporary resolution and (at least temporarily) masking the tensions between or among incommensurable values.

Incommensurable values may also produce "verboten goals" (Yanow, 1996b): goals that are known (sometimes tacitly) and shared, and yet for which explicit, consensual, collective, public support is lacking. Were these verboten goals to be spoken and discussed publicly, public turmoil would result. In diverting attention from incommensurables, myths create areas of silence in public discourse, often around what turn out to be central policy issues, such as these goals. Despite the silences in public discourse, the underlying norms and incommensurable values and beliefs are often known, albeit tacitly. The tacit knowledge is also often communicated: this is accomplished through its symbolic representations, including those in rituals. This is one of the senses in which rituals may be said to enact myths.

What is not said, the silences in discourse based often on assumed and implicit norms, is as deserving of analytic attention as what is said, as postmodernist and feminist analysts have argued. There is a difficulty built in to this sort of analysis: myths divert attention and maintain silences, while the analyst's task is to focus attention on the incommensurables and make the silences speak. Myths of this sort do not exist in a packaged form, waiting for the analyst to uncover and disclose them. As with "ritual," "myth" is analytic language. Because they are so deeply embedded in a polity's or agency's architecture of meaning, the estrangement that the interpretive analyst brings stands her in better stead to examine the many artifactual elements of the policy issue arena from the position of a "nonbeliever."

Someone more imbued with the values, beliefs, and feelings surrounding the policy issue would be much less likely to see its myths. The analyst looks for contradictions between beliefs, values, and/or feelings stated in documents and interviews and those conveyed through acts. She stands as an interpreting, translating Janus figure, conceptually moving back and forth between the local knowledge of policy-relevant publics and the analytic distance of the stranger.

In the example of race-ethnic related policies, I discovered a contradiction between Census Bureau and EEOC policies concerning race-ethnic identity. The Census Bureau tells the enumerator to identify Mary according to what Mary tells him, but the EEOC tells Mary's employer to identify Mary without asking her, according to how she is perceived in the community.[7] (Other agencies' policies and procedures also require race-ethnic identification to be done by others.) These reflect and enact two conflicting senses of race-ethnic identity: an individualistic, subjectivized one and an essentialist, objectivized one, both established by the central government (through the agencies that act in its name and, thereby, on its behalf). As I reflected on agency documents, newspaper articles and books on race-ethnic identity, and directed conversations with Americans of various race-ethnic backgrounds, I came to see a framework of meaning within which both policies made sense. To deflect attention from these incommensurable beliefs, another cherished American cultural value is invoked: the right to individual choice. The census allows Mary to name her race-ethnic identity, but it selects and specifies the categories from which she may choose. What might be called this "choice myth" diverts attention not only from the problematics of subjective versus essentialist race-ethnic identity, but also from the discreteness and "accuracy" of the categories themselves, as noted in Chapter 3.

To return one last time to the example of the ICCC, its ritual of asking annually about its goals is the enactment of what I called, analytically, the "myth of rational goal-setting." I came to this analysis while trying to figure out why an agency would constantly hold public discussions about its goal-setting. It began to make sense when I considered the nature of the policy goals the agency was charged with implementing and its translation of those goals into objectives, programs, and practices over its first decade of operations. The agency had been created in 1969 to narrow a social gap between two major population subgroups, but that gap was no narrower in 1980 than it had been in 1970, judging from reports on income levels, employment, and social status; ethnic tensions and crowded housing conditions were as severe in 1991 as they had been in the 1970s. Agency goals were identified in its literature as achieving social integration, advancing weak communities, and providing quality of life. But such goals are diffuse and their achievement is difficult to measure. Sustaining an organization over a lengthy period without being able to point to progress in goal attainment can be difficult, both for motivating personnel and for reassuring legislators and potentially skeptical publics. The ritual of setting goals, and deriving objectives from them and a plan of operations from the objectives, deflects attention from the goals themselves and their problematic attainment, to the process of setting goals rationally. The ritual of asking "What are our goals?" underscored the belief that agency activities were goal-oriented, communicating to members and stakeholders that the organization is a modern, rational organization doing its work properly, even if accomplishment of those goals is difficult to demonstrate. The ritual enacts the myth of rational goal-setting.

At the same time as the appearance of rational, goal-oriented behavior grants an agency legitimacy and public support, it also creates a conceptual buffer between the administrative goal-setting activity and the agency's technical operations, which serves to put the latter beyond the public's inspection. In analyzing public expectations of schools, Meyer, Scott, and Deal (1977) also discerned such a process. Public schools must appear to carry out societally-mandated "rules" in order to garner public support and legitimacy. Meyer and colleagues found that the technical aspects of schooling—curriculum and teaching—were less important than administrative actions in shaping beliefs about the success of schools (and the professionalization of schools has also removed these technical areas from the public's purview). This gave the analysts a way of explaining why the organizational structures of schools have been "de-coupled" from the technology of schooling.[8]

In the ICCC, the myth reconciles temporarily the tension between two incommensurables: the value of maintaining organizational existence, which requires (among other things) that the agency demonstrate success in achieving its goals, and the value of the policy-related goals themselves, which cannot be demonstrably achieved by this agency with its limited resources, through no fault of its own commission. By directing attention to the processes of goal-setting, the myth diverts attention from the conflict between members' desires to achieve explicit agency goals and the impossibility of their doing so.

Myth analysis, then, may be useful when the researcher-analyst discovers a puzzle or discrepancy between the meanings of two policy-related acts, or between the meanings of acts and language or objects. In reflecting on this puzzle and seeking ways in which the various aspects of it make sense in the policy context, the researcher-analyst may draw on all of the data accessed through observing, participating, interviewing, and analyzing documents, in all of their forms. Such analysis is like a jigsaw puzzle with 1,000 pieces: there is much to fit together, and it can take time. Unlike the puzzle, there is no picture to follow, nor is there any guarantee that a picture will emerge; but if one does, it will be of the analyst's construction out of her familiarity with local knowledge, rather than a preexisting truth discovered on the analytic path.

NOTES

1. Nonverbal communication also falls into the category of symbolic acts: choice of dress, posture, gesture, tone of voice, and so forth at the individual level have their organizational or institutional counterparts in rituals and myths enacted by groups. Others have focused on the meanings of human acts drawing in particular on the metaphor of drama and theater. See, e.g., the work of Arnold (1935, 1937, on the courts and law as drama), Burke (1969, on settings and acts), Edelman (1964, 1988, on politicians' acts), and Goffman (1959, on front stage and backstage in everyday life).

2. This example is based on Buckle, Thomas-Buckle, Cook, and Yanow (1984).

3. Organizational analysts, in particular, have also used the terms "ceremony," "rite," and "play" to refer to aspects of the same phenomenon. These are found in organizational life in award ceremonies, holiday celebrations, retirement dinners, training programs, and so forth. On the subject of myths, ceremonies, rituals, play, and so on in organizational and governmental life, see Floden and Weiner (1978), Handelman (1976), Harris and Sutton (1986), Meyer and Rowan (1983), Robertson (1980), Trice and Beyer (1993, pp. 107-127), and Westerlund and Sjostrand (1979). There has been considerable attention given to elections and television as contexts for rituals and ceremonies. See, for example, Edelman (1988) and Nimmo and Combs (1980). Seeing "play" in organizational life as one way in which tacitly known meanings are communicated has led to a reexamination of the roles of humor, jokes, gossip, and so forth (see, for example, Handelman, 1976), as well as to a critical assessment of the absence of emotion and sexuality in academic studies of worklife and of attempts to suppress them in practice (see, for example, Hearn et al., 1990). Bell (1997, chaps. 1-3) provides an excellent summary of the history of ideas concerning ritual.

4. The following discussion is condensed from Yanow (1996b, chap. 7).

5. This is in keeping with postmodernist notions of identity as well as feminist standpoint theories of identity.

6. There is a long theoretical history, especially in studies of religion, of treating ritual and myth together, including arguments about which took precedence over the other, either in historical development or in power. Bell (1997, chap. 1) details this history. My own approach is to treat them as intertwined, with neither predominating. The discussion that follows is based on Yanow (1996b, chap. 7).

7. In practice the distinction is not quite so stark: the Census Bureau treats answers according to rules of statistical significance, at times regrouping individuals' answers, as when it sought to amalgamate Asian and Pacific Islanders, Native Americans, and Whites into a single category for analysis in certain geographic areas after the 1990 census, because the separate counts were statistically insignificant. There is also some indication that EEOC implementation differs from policy.

8. Manning (1977) makes a similar observation: "It is not surprising that organizations of central symbolic importance should call upon the legitimating powers of the myth of rationality to justify both their existence and actions." See also Ingersoll and Adams (1992) on the "rational technical myth system" and Westerlund and Sjostrand (1979, pp. 36-42) on the myth of rational goals.

6. MOVING FROM FIELDWORK AND DESKWORK TO TEXTWORK AND BEYOND

It would be very easy to get lost in the intricacies of the analytic approaches presented in the last three chapters. The researcher-analyst has to move from the details of these analytic processes to the policy meanings being communicated, much as she moved from the details of observation and interviewing while accessing data to their analysis. These several activities can now be conceptually joined as an extended analytic process, as illustrated in Figure 6.1, which modifies the traditional presentation of the course of scientific research.

Note the many areas of overlap: deskwork (establishing the analytic question, designing the study, analyzing accessed data) often takes place while fieldwork (identifying interpretive communities and symbolic artifacts, accessing data) is in progress, especially in a policy situation in which the analyst moves back and forth in a single day between office and field sites; and textwork[1] (report preparation) and deskwork (data analysis) may similarly overlap in time, as writing itself entails analysis.

There are several occasions for iterative loops in this process. Establishing the analytic question both leads to and depends on identifying interpretive communities and symbolic artifacts. In the course of designing a study, including the choice of methods, it may become clear that the analytic question needs to be reconceptualized. Similarly, in beginning to access data, it may also become clear that the research question cannot be explored using those methods or that design, or that the question itself needs to be revised, refined, or reframed. In beginning to analyze data or in preparing the report, the researcher may discover that data are insuffi-

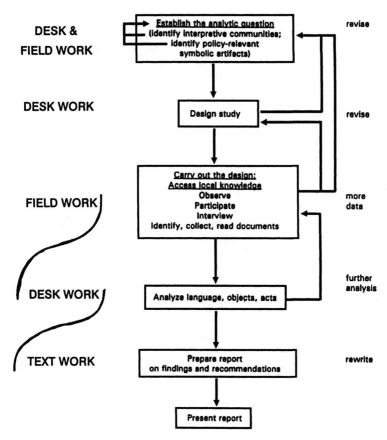

Figure 6.1 The analytic process.

ciently robust to support analysis or that analysis reveals new angles, requiring the accessing of additional data. Upon presenting the report (either oral or written), the analyst may discover the need to begin the process again, by revising the research question or the study design, accessing additional data, analyzing further the existing data, or even by rewriting the report. All these are part of a normal policy analytic process.

What this diagram (Figure 6.1) leaves out, except by implication, is the context of prior knowledge, either of the policy issue in question or of the setting in which the policy has been or is to be enacted: the analytic question emerges out of this, as does the identification of interpretive communities and policy-relevant artifacts. In this sense, analysis really begins with the activities in the third box even before the question or the study design has been formalized. In practice, because they are working in a policy or agency context, analysts begin with a diffuse sense of what the question is and of what the issues are. The first two boxes represent the activities entailed in crystallizing that diffuseness. Here is where academic research often differs: the academic (student or faculty) who chooses a research question without prior experiential or conceptual knowledge of the policy issue begins by building up the a priori knowledge that the practitioner brings with him to the first two steps. This contextual knowledge is often developed through library-based research, conducting informational interviews, reading contemporary and archival media coverage and position papers, and so on. This is in keeping with hermeneutic concepts that envision human reasoning and learning broadly construed as a circle. The researcher-analyst begins the sense-making process wherever he is located on the circle (here, for example, in the midst of observing or studying policy documents). He makes provisional sense, engages in further inquiry, revises his understanding, engages in further inquiry, and so on, moving in a reiterative fashion from field to analysis to question to study design to field to analysis to writing to analysis, and so on. It is in this sense, too, that research produces "findings" rather than "conclusions": what was certain knowledge in 1491 was dethroned soon after. As with all science, interpretive analysis requires a sense of provisional certainty and an attitude of confirmed doubt.

Textwork as World-Making

At last! The fieldwork is done, the data have been accessed and analyzed, and it is time to write out the analysis and one's findings. Where to begin?

There is little guidance on writing policy analytic reports or on how to write any other form of interpretive research. With rare exception,[2] writing processes have been left to a kind of learning-by-doing apprenticeship, whether on the job or in the academy. A journeyman (advanced graduate student in the role of teaching assistant) or master craftsman (experienced analyst or professor, often in the form of journal referee or editor) rejects one's work or calls for revisions (the latter including scribbled marginal comments and final grades). In the next rounds one incorporates prior suggestions, learning in the process the standards of rhetoric, structure, evidence, and voice for particular audiences, readers, and venues (a dissertation vs. a course paper, a journal article vs. a dissertation, an analytic report vs. academic writing). One is (or at least until recently has been) expected to absorb, as if by osmosis, appropriate writing styles and techniques from reading the work of others in one's field (whether academic or applied). Recent developments in narrative analysis applied to the social sciences (see Chapter 3) have begun to make writing matters more explicit. Even so, they are almost nonexistent in the field of public policy; even in organizational studies, they take the form of critique more than of how-to.[3] Due to space limitations, I will address here only one practical aspect of writing, and this one because it ties in to one of the central conceptual issues of interpretive research.

Conversational interviews, observational and participatory activities, and the assessment of documents produce in their wake extensively detailed data and extensive notes on those data. Clearly, the analyst cannot include all of these in her report. How to proceed in the face of such abundance? As with any writing, the researcher-analyst selects from among her data those directly quoted words and phrases and those noted observational details that support the argument she seeks to make in her report. Much (though not necessarily all) of the rest of the data are presented in summary: material from several interviews or from observations of several events is integrated to make a single point ("As five department heads reported . . ."; "On seven different occasions . . ."). What this point (or set of points) is emerges from reading and rereading and rereading again the interview transcripts, observational records, and documents that one has prepared and brought from field to desk. These are typically stored in files, although occasionally it is appropriate to append a transcript or one or more documents to a report (depending on the context).

This selectivity and summarizing mean that the researcher-analyst is not producing a mirror image or tape recording of what he or she saw and heard. Instead, he or she is contributing to shaping the way the policy issue is perceived and acted on. The written (or oral) report is itself a form of *worldmaking* (in Nelson Goodman's [1978] phrase), and in it the researcher-analyst's own interpretive frame or lens is embedded. Even when the author chooses such techniques as the use of the passive voice ("is embedded") and the omission of the first person "I," the writing is not "objective," precisely because the author has selected what features of the study to present and is using various rhetorical devices to persuade the reader of the scientific trustworthiness of the report.

In giving up the position of positive knowledge, one of the thornier problems in interpretive analysis emerges: when the actor's sensemaking and the researcher-analyst's analysis of the same situation conflict. Interpretive philosophies require the researcher-analyst to pursue the meaning for the actor in the situation. But as a participant-observer, the researcher is also an actor in the situation. Should the researcher's meaning-making be subordinated to that of the "real" actor?

On hearing an actor's or reader's interpretation, the researcher-analyst may conclude that her interpretation was wrong—the actor presents enough supporting data to persuade her that she misunderstood—and she revises her report. There are other times when conflicting interpretations cannot be reconciled so easily; in practice, some policy debates are intractable to resolution. The analyst can delineate the reasons behind the disagreements and encourage ongoing engaged, passionate discussion. She may choose to include the dissenting interpretation(s) in the report, either in the text or in a note. This is the practical implication of a democratic analytic process that accords actors' local knowledge the status of expertise (in the lived experience of local conditions), alongside the analytic expertise of the policy analyst. In a narrative sense, this constitutes the joint production of an understanding of the policy situation.

Issues in the Practice and Teaching of Interpretive Analysis

An aspect of policy making emerges in interpretive policy analysis, which is not evident in more traditional approaches. Taken together, policy artifacts and their multiple meanings can be read as expressions of identity on the part of the polity that legislated them. As mentioned in Chapter 4, these "identity stories" are ways in which the polity—be it local, state, regional, or national—tells its own citizens and often citizens of other polities, including extranational ones, who it is, in terms of what it values, believes, or feels. Whereas traditional approaches to policy analysis focus on policies as exclusively instrumental and goal-oriented, interpretive approaches add the expressive dimension of human policy-making action, demonstrating and enacting for a variety of audiences, near and far, what a polity finds meaningful.

My favorite example comes from the realm of nuclear policy. The cities of Berkeley, Oakland, Hayward, and Santa Cruz, all in California, as well as Cambridge, Massachusetts, Ann Arbor, Michigan, and others, have passed legislation declaring themselves "nuclear-free zones." In the California cities, signs proclaiming this status are posted along most city streets. Yet nuclear materials are shipped on federal highways, and federal law supersedes local law. Therefore, these cities cannot stop nuclear materials from entering the zones they have declared off limits. Why legislate a policy that is so clearly unimplementable? An instrumental approach would be hard pressed to answer this; even theorists as sensitive to the multivocality of policy mandates as Jeffrey Pressman and Aaron Wildavsky wrote, there is "no point in having good ideas if they can't be carried out" (1984, p. 143). Yet from an interpretive vantage point, the reason seems clear: precisely because of the expressive aspect of human action, because public policies are also ways in which we tell group identity stories.

Kristen Luker (1984) provides an extended example from the contentions over abortion policy. The debate, she notes, is not about "facts" but rather about what those facts mean. Those meanings are the grounds through which arguments about personhood are being worked out, and these include representations of different worldviews entailing beliefs, values, and feelings and their attendant social realities. In this sense, policy recommendations are collective expressions of individuals' identities, articulated in and through groups; and efforts to get the state to endorse one view represent not just a potential victory of material resources (to implement that view) but also a public endorsement of that collective identity as the polity's identity. Gusfield's (1963) account of Prohibition and Repeal similarly illustrates a policy battle not just for the instrumental regulation of the consumption of alcohol, but also for the expression of national identity in the form of one set of religious, social, class, and moral ideas, a victory of one group's identity over that of another.

That is not to say that policies are either instrumental or expressive. Often they are both. In New Zealand, for example, antinuclear demonstrations in Auckland and elsewhere also ended up swaying the newly elected Prime Minister to an antinuclear position, as a consequence of which French nuclear ships were denied permission to enter and dock at Auckland's harbor.[4] U.S. immigration policy, to take another example, is clearly instrumental: it is designed to regulate the number and type of people allowed into the United States. Yet it is also expressive: it is one way in which American citizens tell ourselves, potential immigrants, and foreign governments and their residents who we are as a nation and what our shared values, beliefs, and feelings are. It is in no small part due to this expressive dimension that immigration policy is so highly contested today, as it has been at other key points in our past. If the "English only" movement succeeds, there will be instrumental consequences for school curricula and governmental forms; but there are meaningful, expressive reasons for its resurgence and strength at this point in time that may affect not only its drafting but also its potential legislative path and implementation career, and a policy analyst would want not only to be aware of these possibilities but also to have methods for accessing and analyzing them.

What does this mean for the role of the policy analyst?

Traditionally, policy analysis has been taught and presented as the dispassionate exercise of technocratic expertise based on a value-free position. This is the pursuit of policy analysis under the influence of the standards of reason and science invoked by the canons of 19th- and 20th-century positivism and logical positivism. The phenomenological and hermeneutic philosophies that underpin interpretive approaches, by contrast, assume a situated knower: an analyst whose interpretation is shaped by prior education and training, family and communal background, societal position, and experience, whose knowledge constitutes a frame itself. Neither this person nor the knowledge he possesses is or can be objective: there is no point of view outside the matter being studied from which to observe it; following Heisenberg's uncertainty principle in physics, acts of observation themselves affect that which is being observed. In this sense, analysis—although made dispassionately, with reason and logic—is not and cannot be value-free.[5] It is not adequate to say, along the lines of one response of policy analysis to this critique, I'll make my values or bias explicit up front and then proceed with objective, dispassionate analysis. As Hawkesworth (1988, pp. 58-61) carefully argues, this is philosophically and logically not possible.

On the other hand, it is not necessary within an interpretive practice for the policy analyst to adopt an advocacy position (Peattie, 1968). Although that may conceptually address the recognition that policy analysts are not free of values and biases, it is not the only option available to an interpretive analyst.

Rather, the interpretive policy analyst can be seen as a translator, bringing other interpretive communities' stories to her employing policymaker, agency, or community group, helping each to understand the stories of the others. The task of policy analysis in this view is to identify and to explain "the diverse dimensions of debate pertinent to particular policy questions" (Hawkesworth, 1988, p. 94), enabling a more informed policy deliberation and choice. Interpretive policy analysts, whatever their particular analytic methods, by and large share the intention to involve and make speak as many voices in the policy conversation as possible. Roe (1994) presents several examples of this sort of policy analytic practice, working in one case with the University of California at Berkeley and California Indian groups around conflicting ideas about ownership and display of Indian artifacts. This required him to access the local knowledge of each interpretive community and to translate between them. The whole point of an interpretive approach to policy analysis, to paraphrase Clifford Geertz, is "to aid . . . in gaining access to the conceptual world in which [policy actors] live so that [all] can, in some extended sense of the term, converse with [one another]" (1973, p. 24). Accessing and analyzing local knowledge is what the analyst does to prepare for and assist in such conversations and translations:

- Learning the "vocabulary" and "rules of grammar" of the various interpretive communities.
- Identifying and learning the meanings of policy-relevant symbolic artifacts in the "language" of each community.
- Learning to speak like a member of each community, without necessarily becoming one.

In other words, the analyst learns to make sense of a situation from different angles and brings that sensemaking to others. The analyst "travels" to other policy-relevant interpretive communities and tells (or enables the telling of) other communities' stories, facilitating their understanding. It is a role that is at once translator and mediator.[6]

This approach is more democratic than traditional policy analytic approaches, as noted earlier, in two senses. Interpretive analysis depends on the policy analyst's skills as translator-storyteller, not as technocratic expert, thereby opening up the conversation to "lay" people (who are often the ones affected by the policy issue) and short-circuiting the contemporary societal value placed on science and its technical language. It is also democratic in that it relies on the presence of multiple stories, told from the points of view of, ideally, all policy-relevant actors, and not only on the stories (and thereby values) of experts, policymakers, or other elites.

That such an approach is practical and not just utopian can be seen in an example from the domain of science and technology policy. In the early-to mid-1970s, biologists developed the process known as "recombinant DNA" (rDNA), the ability to cut and splice genes, recombining parts of some with pieces of other cut genes. This was at once hailed as a new technique and held in suspicion by scientists themselves. Prosecution of rDNA research was restricted to labs with top level security construction and protocols. In 1975 scientists called for a moratorium on further research until the implications of rDNA could be studied. In 1976 the Cambridge, Massachusetts, city council held two open hearings, voting for a three-month moratorium on research requiring the top two security levels.[7]

At its July 7 meeting, the council also voted to establish a Cambridge Experimentation Review Board (CERB) to advise the council on such policy issues. When appointed, its nine members included two doctors, two former city councilors, a structural engineer, a university administrator/ academic, and a civic leader, none of whom had any direct experience with rDNA research. After requesting, and getting, a three-month extension on the city moratorium, the CERB delivered a report recommending that the research be allowed to proceed. The CERB and its report were hailed nationally and locally by university scientists, science reporters, and civic leaders (except for the mayor of Cambridge and one city councilor) for their fair and informed work, especially given their lay status on the subject. Citizens who otherwise might not have been represented in policy debates were intentionally and concertedly made central to the policy analytic process through the actions of the mayor and members of the city council.

The normative position to which many in the interpretive policy analysis world subscribe is that policy analysts have a responsibility to make silenced stories and silenced communities speak: to bring them, their values, and their points of view to the conversation. It may be more difficult to identify unspoken stories and the interpretive communities whose meanings are not included in issue discourse, especially since these are typically the ones who lack the power (including organizing abilities) to get their views heard. The difficulty may be enhanced, for instance, by the formal organizational position of the policy analyst serving as a member of government rather than as an independent researcher with an academic base. Local knowledge is more easily accessed where it "resides"; the difficulties of implementing this approach need to be grappled with, and the critique should not stop us from trying to identify all the actors and include their stories.

Many also come to argue for some form of "passionate humility" (Yanow, 1997)—the conviction that one is right coupled with the possibility that one might be wrong—as a counterweight to the stance of technocratic expertise. Michael McCoy (1996) and Jeanette Hofmann (1996) talk about this as the need for the analyst to listen: recognizing the existence and importance of local knowledge shifts the sense of "expert" away from the analyst. Roe (1994), invoking Isaiah Berlin, calls for humility in the face of the pluralism of incommensurable values that characterizes the policy world, which "speaks to tolerance in the face of uncertainty" (p. 19).

Students in policy analysis graduate programs in political science, public policy, and administrative science, who are largely still being trained exclusively in positivist modes of thought and methods of analysis, are often surprised when they discover the limits of traditional approaches in the midst of field research. Jeanette Hofmann, for example, reports on her discovery that the businesspeople she interviewed talked about technology transfer in terms that did not fit the policy model she was investigating and had been led to believe was accurate, and on her surprise that the difference was a matter of interpretation rather than "fact." The research approach she used, and her theoretical constructs, emerged as an "unintended by-product in the course of field research." Hal Colebatch's story is similar: the experienced realities of multiple interpretations in local government practice did not fit the anticipated model of a single, universally valid, explanatory truth. He notes the similarity to his own experience of Deborah Stone's (1988) reflection that she did not begin her critique of the market model of policy analysis from any particular "ism"—although in both cases it is possible to find ex post facto affinities to various forms of interpretive analysis.[8] What these and others' experiences suggest is that it is time to (re)integrate the philosophy of (social) science into methods courses, so that epistemological and ontological concerns are once again joined with their related methodological concerns. If this were done, methods choices would be less likely to limit the kinds of analytic and research questions that are asked.

The examples of analysis presented here show that "interpretation" does not mean "impressionistic," as I noted in Chapter 1. The hallmarks of science, as Pal (1996) has observed, are "reflexivity about methods, a systematic approach, the greatest reliance possible on logic in persuasion and argument, and usually (though not always) some measure of empirical observation." Although they do not follow the stepwise fashion of decision or regression analysis, metaphor, category, space, ritual, and myth analysis, as well as observation, participation, conversational interviewing, and document analysis, have their own logic and systematicness. The data accessing methods of observation and interviewing recognize that human acts and responses cannot be regulated and controlled, and there is much to learn about policy action that lab experimentation cannot garner. Interpretive methods build in and on human variability among actors and researchers alike and thereby facilitate not just a gathering of facts, but an insight into what those "facts" mean.

NOTES

1. I have borrowed this term from Van Maanen (1996).
2. See Becker (1986) for one effort.
3. But see Gusfield (1976, 1981) for exceptions in public policy, written by a sociologist, and Golden-Biddle and Locke (1997) for exceptions in organizational studies.

94

4. I owe this example to Ray Nairn, Senior Lecturer in Psychology, Auckland University (personal communication, July 1995).

5. See also Rein (1976) on this, as well as Hawkesworth's (1988) excellent critique.

6. I had originally included the word "educator" here as well but have removed it following Peter Plug's observation (personal communication, 1997) that "educator" often "implies that the policy analyst is 'wiser'" than members of interpretive communities and in a position to teach them, whereas "it is actually the policy analyst who has something to learn" from them.

7. This example is based on Yanow (1985).

8. Both Hofmann's and Colebatch's observations were included in earlier versions of the essays published in 1995.

REFERENCES

Abma, T. A. (1997). Powerful stories: About the role of stories in sustaining and transforming the professional practice within a mental hospital. *Beleid & Maatschappij 1*, 5.

Abma, T. A. (Ed.). (in press). Telling tales: On narrative and evaluation. In *Advances in Program Evaluation: Vol. 6*. Greenwich, CT: JAI.

Appleyard, D. (1981). *Livable streets*. Berkeley: University of California Press.

Argyris, C., & Schon, D. A. (1974). *Theory in practice*. San Francisco: Jossey-Bass.

Arnold, T. (1935). *The symbols of government*. New Haven: Yale University Press.

Arnold, T. (1937). *The folklore of capitalism*. New Haven: Yale University Press.

Ascher, W. (1987). Editorial: Political sciences and the economic approach in a "post-positivist" era. *Policy Sciences, 20*, 3-9.

Baier, V. E., March, J. G., & Saetren, H. (1986). Implementation and ambiguity. *Scandinavian Journal of Management Studies, 2*, 197-212.

Bateson, G. (1955). *Steps to an ecology of mind*. New York: Ballantine.

Becker, H. (1986). *Writing for social scientists*. Chicago: University of Chicago Press.

Bell, C. (1997). *Ritual*. New York: Oxford University Press.

Berger, P. L., & Luckmann, T. (1966). *The social construction of reality*. New York: Anchor.

Bernstein, B. (1977). Ritual in education. In B. Bernstein (Ed.), *Class, codes, and control: Vol. 3* (2nd ed., pp. 54-66). Boston: Routledge & Kegan Paul.

Bernstein, R. J. (1976). *The restructuring of social and political theory*. Philadelphia: University of Pennsylvania Press.

Bernstein, R. J. (1983). *Beyond objectivism and relativism*. Philadelphia: University of Pennsylvania Press.

Black, M. (1962). *Models and metaphors*. Ithaca, NY: Cornell University Press.

Bonser, C. F., McGregor, E. B., Jr., & Oster, C. V., Jr. (1996). *Policy choices and public action*. Englewood Cliffs, NJ: Prentice Hall.

Brown, R. H. (1976). Social theory as metaphor. *Theory and Society, 3*, 169-197.

Bruner, J. (1990). *Acts of meaning*. Cambridge: Harvard University Press.

Brunner, R. D. (1982). The policy sciences as science. *Policy Sciences, 15*, 115-135.

Brunner, R. D. (1987). Key political symbols. *Policy Sciences, 20*, 53-76.

Buckle, L. G., Thomas-Buckle, S. R., Cook, S., & Yanow, D. (1984, January). *Evaluation of the* [name deleted] *environmental mediation center*. Unpublished report.

Buker, E. (1987). *Through a looking glass: Understanding political cultures through structuralist interpretations of narratives.* Westport, CT: Greenwood.

Bulmer, M. (1986). The value of qualitative methods. In M. Bulmer (Ed.), *Social science and social policy* (pp. 180-203). Boston: Allen and Unwin.

Burke, K. (1969). *A grammar of motives.* Berkeley: University of California Press. (original work published 1945)

Burrell, G., & Morgan, G. (1979). *Sociological paradigms and organisational analysis.* Exeter, NH: Heinemann.

Charon, J. M. (1985). *Symbolic interactionism* (2nd ed.). Englewood Cliffs, NJ: Prentice Hall.

Chock, P. P. (1995). Ambiguity in policy discourse: Congressional talk about immigration. *Policy Sciences, 18*(2), 165-184.

Cicourel, A. V. (1964). *Method and measurement in sociology.* New York: Free Press.

Clifford, J. (1988). *The predicament of culture.* Cambridge: Harvard University Press.

Colebatch, H. K. (1995). Organizational meanings of program evaluation. *Policy Sciences, 18*(2), 149-164.

Czarniawska-Joerges, B. (1992). Budgets as texts: On collective writing in the public sector. *Accounting, Management & Information Technology, 2*(4), 221-239.

Czarniawska-Joerges, B. (1993). Stories of transformation in public administration. In R. Larsson, L. Bengtsson, K. Eneroth, & A. T. Malm (Eds.), *Research in Strategic Change.* Lund, Sweden: Lund University Press.

Czarniawska-Joerges, B., & Guillet de Monthoux, P. (1994). *Good novels, better management: Reading organizational realities in fiction.* Chur, Switzerland: Harwood.

Dallmayr, F. R., & McCarthy, T. A. (Eds.). (1977). *Understanding and social inquiry.* Notre Dame, IN: University of Notre Dame Press.

Darnton, R. (1984). *The great cat massacre and other episodes in French cultural history.* New York: Basic Books.

Davis, N. Z. (1983). *The return of Martin Guerre.* Cambridge: Harvard University Press.

Deal, T. E., & Kennedy, A. A. (1982). *Corporate cultures.* Reading, MA: Addison-Wesley.

DeHaven-Smith, L. (1988). *Philosophical critiques of policy analysis.* Gainesville: University of Florida Press.

Dery, D. (1987). Knowing: The political way. *Policy Studies Review, 7*(1), 13-25.

Douglas, M. (1966). *Purity and danger.* London: Routledge & Kegan Paul.

Douglas, M. (1975). *Implicit meanings.* London: Routledge & Kegan Paul.

Douglas, M. (1982). *Natural symbols.* New York: Pantheon. (Original work published 1973)

Dryzek, J. S. (1982). Policy analysis as a hermeneutic activity. *Policy Sciences, 14,* 309-329.

Edelman, M. (1964). *The symbolic uses of politics.* Urbana: University of Illinois Press.

Edelman, M. (1971). *Politics as symbolic action.* Chicago: Markham.

Edelman, M. (1977). *Political language.* New York: Academic Press.

Edelman, M. (1988). *Constructing the political spectacle.* Chicago: University of Chicago Press.

Edelman, M. (1995). *Art and politics.* Chicago: University of Chicago Press.

Erlandson, D. A., Harris, E. L., Skipper, B. L., & Allen, S. D. (1993). *Doing naturalistic inquiry.* Newbury Park, CA: Sage.

Fay, B. (1975). *Social theory and political practice.* Boston: George Allen & Unwin.

Feldman, M. S. (1988). *Order without design.* Stanford, CA: Stanford University Press.

Feldman. M. S. (1994). *Some interpretive techniques for analyzing qualitative data.* Newbury Park, CA: Sage.

Filmer, P., Phillipson, M., Silverman, D., & Walsh, D. (1972). *New directions in sociological theory.* London: Collier-Macmillan.

Fischer, F. (1980). Critical evaluation of public policy. In J. Forester (Ed.), *Critical theory and public life* (pp. 231-257). Cambridge: MIT Press.

Fischer, F. (1990). *Technocracy and the politics of expertise.* Newbury Park, CA: Sage.

Fischer, F. (1995). *Evaluating public policy.* Chicago: Nelson-Hall.

Fischer, F., & Forester, J. (Eds.). (1993). *The argumentative turn in policy analysis and planning.* Durham, NC: Duke University Press.

Fish, S. (1980). *Is there a text in this class? The authority of interpretive communities.* Cambridge: Harvard University Press.

Floden, R. E., & Weiner, S. S. (1978). Rationality to ritual: The multiple roles of evaluation in governmental processes. *Policy Sciences, 9,* 9-18.

Fried, M. (1963). Grieving for a lost home. In L. J. Duhl (Ed.), *The urban condition.* New York: Basic Books.

Gagliardi, P. (1990). Artifacts as pathways and remains of organizational life. In P. Gagliardi (Ed.), *Symbols and artifacts* (pp. 3-38). New York: Aldine de Gruyter.

Gans, H. (1976). Personal Journal: B. On the methods used in this study. In M. P. Golden (Ed.), *The research experience* (pp. 49-59). Itasca IL: F. E. Peacock.

Garfinkel, H. (1977). What is ethnomethodology? In F. R. Dallmayr & T. A. McCarthy (Eds.), *Understanding and social inquiry* (pp. 240-261). Notre Dame, IN: University of Notre Dame Press.

Geertz, C. (1973). *The interpretation of cultures.* New York: Basic Books.

Geertz, C. (1983). *Local knowledge.* New York: Basic Books.

Geertz, C. (1988). *Works and lives.* Stanford, CA: Stanford University Press.

Goffman, E. (1959). *The presentation of self in everyday life.* New York: Doubleday Anchor.

Goffman, E. (1974). *Frame analysis.* New York: Harper & Row.

Goffman, E. (1979). *Gender advertisements.* Cambridge: Harvard University Press.

Golden-Biddle, K., & Locke, K. (1993). Appealing work: An investigation in how ethnographic texts convince. *Organization Science, 4*(4), 595-616.

Golden-Biddle, K., & Locke, K. (1997). *Composing qualitative research.* Thousand Oaks, CA: Sage.

Goodman, N. (1978). *Ways of worldmaking.* Indianapolis: Hackett.

Goodsell, C. (1988). *The social meaning of civic space.* Lawrence: University Press of Kansas.

Goodsell, C. (Ed.). (1993). Architectural settings of governance. [Special issue]. *Journal of Architectural and Planning Research, 10*(4).

Guba, E. G., & Lincoln, Y. S. (1989). *Fourth generation evaluation.* Newbury Park, CA: Sage.

Gusfield, J. (1976). The literary rhetoric of science. *American Sociological Review, 41,* 16-34.

Gusfield, J. R. (1963). *Symbolic crusade.* Urbana: University of Illinois Press.

Gusfield, J. R. (1981). *The culture of public problems.* Chicago: University of Chicago Press.

Habermas, J. (1987). *The theory of communicative action* (T. McCarthy, Trans.). Boston: Beacon.

Hall, E. T. (1959). *The silent language*. New York: Anchor Books.

Hall, E. T. (1966). *The hidden dimension*. New York: Doubleday.

Halprin, L. (1972). *Cities* (Rev. ed.). Cambridge: MIT Press.

Hammersley, M. (1993). *What's wrong with ethnography?* London: Sage.

Handelman, D. (1976). Re-thinking 'Banana Time.' *Urban Life, 4*(4), 433-448.

Harris, S. G., & Sutton, R. I. (1986). Functions of parting ceremonies in dying organizations. *Academy of Management Journal, 29*(1), 5-30.

Hatch, M. J. (1993). The dynamics of organizational culture. *Academy of Management Review, 18*(4), 657-693.

Hatch, M. J. (1996). The role of the researcher: An analysis of narrative position in organization theory. *Journal of Management Inquiry, 5*(4), 359-374.

Hatch, M. J. (1997). *Organization theory*. New York: Oxford University Press.

Hawkesworth, M. E. (1988). *Theoretical issues in policy analysis*. Albany: SUNY Press.

Healy, P. (1986). Interpretive policy inquiry. *Policy Sciences, 19*, 381-396.

Hearn, J., Sheppard, D., Sheriff-Tancred, P., & Burrell, G. (1990). *The sexuality of organization*. Newbury Park, CA: Sage.

Heineman, R. A., Bluhm, W. T., Peterson, S. A., & Kearny, E. N. (1990). *The world of the policy analyst*. Chatham, NJ: Chatham House.

Hofmann, J. (1995). Implicit theories in policy discourse: Interpretations of reality in German technology policy. *Policy Sciences, 18*(2), 127-148.

Hofmann, J. (1996, March). *Making paradoxes productive: The unexpected as signposts in empirical research*. Paper presented at the Western Political Science Association Annual Conference, San Francisco.

Holstein, J. A., & Gubrium, J. F. (1995). *The active interview*. Thousand Oaks, CA: Sage.

Hood, C., & Jackson, M. (1994). Keys for locks in administrative argument. *Administration & Society, 25*(4), 467-488.

Hubbard, R. (1989). Science, facts, and feminism. In N. Tuana (Ed.), *Feminism & science*. Bloomington: Indiana University Press.

Hunter, A. (1974). *Symbolic communities*. Chicago: University of Chicago Press.

Ingersoll, V. H., & Adams, G. B. (1992). *The tacit organization*. Greenwich, CT: JAI.

Iser, W. (1989). *Prospecting: From reader response to literary anthropology*. Baltimore: Johns Hopkins University Press.

Israel Corporation of Community Centers. (1971). *Community centers in Israel*. Jerusalem: Author.

Jackson, J. B. (1980). *The necessity for ruins and other topics*. Amherst: University of Massachusetts Press.

Jennings, B. (1983). Interpretive social science and policy analysis. In D. Callahan & B. Jennings (Eds.), *Ethics, the social sciences, and policy analysis* (pp. 3-35). New York: Plenum.

Jennings, B. (1987). Interpretation and the practice of policy analysis. In F. Fischer & J. Forester (Eds.), *Confronting values in policy analysis* (pp. 128-152). Newbury Park, CA: Sage.

Kaplan, T. J. (1986). The narrative structure of policy analysis. *Journal of Policy Analysis and Management, 5*(4), 761-778.

Karp, I., & Lavine, S. D. (1991). *Exhibiting cultures*. Washington, DC: Smithsonian Press.

Kelly, R. M. (1987). The politics of meaning and policy inquiry. In D. J. Palumbo (Ed.), *The politics of program evaluation* (Chap. 10). Newbury Park, CA: Sage.

98

Kuhn, T. S. (1962). *The structure of scientific revolutions.* Chicago: University of Chicago Press.

Kunda, G. (1992). *Engineering culture.* Philadelphia: Temple University Press.

Lakoff, G. (1987). *Women, fire, and dangerous things.* Chicago: University of Chicago Press.

Lakoff, G. (1996). *Moral politics: What conservatives know that liberals don't.* Chicago: University of Chicago Press.

Lakoff, G., & Johnson, M. (1980). *Metaphors we live by.* Chicago: University of Chicago Press.

Lakoff, G., & Johnson, M. (1987). The metaphorical logic of rape. *Metaphor and Symbolic Activity, 2*(1), 73-79.

Langer, S. K. (1957). *Philosophy in a new key* (3rd ed.). Cambridge: Harvard University Press.

Lasswell, H. D. (1979). *The signature of power.* New Brunswick, NJ: Transaction Publishing.

Lasswell, H. D., Leites, N., & Associates. (1949). *The language of politics.* Cambridge: MIT Press.

Lasswell, H. D., Lerner, D., & De Sola Pool, I. (1952). *The comparative study of symbols.* Stanford, CA: The Hoover Institute.

Lather, P. (1986). Research as praxis. *Harvard Educational Review, 56*(30), 257-277.

Latour, B. (1987). *Science in action.* Cambridge: Harvard University Press.

Lave, J., & Wenger, E. (1991). *Situated learning.* New York: Cambridge University Press.

Lavi, Z. (1979). A venture born under Gemini. In *Summaries and objectives: 1969-1979* (pp. 8-14) [Hebrew with English summary]. Jerusalem: Israel Corporation of Community Centers.

Lindblom, C. E., & Cohen, D. K. (1979). *Usable knowledge.* New Haven, CT: Yale University Press.

Linde, C. (1993). *Life stories: The creation of coherence.* New York: Oxford University Press.

Linder, S. H. (1995). Contending discourses in the electromagnetic fields controversy. *Policy Sciences, 18*(2), 209-230.

Lipsky, M. (1979). *Street-level bureaucracy.* New York: Russell Sage.

Luker, K. (1984). *Abortion and the politics of motherhood.* Berkeley: University of California Press.

Lynch, K. (1960). *The image of the city.* Cambridge: MIT Press.

Lynch, K. (1972). *What time is this place?* Cambridge: MIT Press.

Manning, P. (1977, November). *Resources, information and strategy.* Paper presented to the American Society of Criminology, Atlanta, GA.

Marcus, G. E., & Fischer, M. (1986). *Anthropology as cultural critique.* Chicago: University of Chicago Press.

Maynard-Moody, S. (1993). Stories managers tell. In B. Bozeman (Ed.), *Public management.* San Francisco: Jossey-Bass.

Maynard-Moody, S., & Stull, D. (1987). The symbolic side of policy analysis. In F. Fischer & J. Forester (Eds.), *Confronting values in policy analysis* (chap. 11). Newbury Park, CA: Sage.

McCloskey, D. (1985). *The rhetoric of economics.* Madison: University of Wisconsin Press.

McCoy, M. (1996, March). *Learning to listen: Asking questions from within.* Paper presented to the Western Political Science Association Annual Conference, San Francisco.

McCoy, M. D. (1995). *Domestic politics for international understanding: Chinese sustainable agriculture from an interpretive perspective.* Unpublished doctoral dissertation, Department of Political Science, University of Utah.

McLuhan, M. (1964). *Understanding media.* New York: McGraw-Hill.

Meinig, D. W. (Ed.). (1979). *The interpretation of ordinary landscapes.* New York: Oxford University Press.

Meyer, J. W., & Rowan, B. (1983). Institutionalized organizations: Formal structure as myth and ceremony. In J. W. Meyer & W. R. Scott (Eds.), *Organizational environments* (pp. 21-44). Beverly Hills, CA: Sage.

Meyer, J. W., Scott, R., & Deal, T. (1977). *Research on school and district organization.* Paper presented at Sociology of Education Conference, San Diego, CA.

Miller, D. F. (1982). Metaphor, thinking, and thought. *Et cetera, 39*(2), 134-150.

Miller, D. F. (1985). Social policy: An exercise in metaphor. *Knowledge, 7*(2), 191-215.

Minow, M. (1990). *Making all the difference.* Ithaca, NY: Cornell University Press.

Morgan, G. (1986). *Images of organization.* Beverly Hills, CA: Sage.

Murphy, J. T. (1980). *Getting the facts.* Santa Monica: Goodyear.

Nimmo, D., & Combs, J. E. (1980). *Subliminal politics.* Englewood Cliffs, NJ: Prentice Hall.

O'Connor, E. (1996). Telling decisions: Organizational decision making and narrative construction. In Z. Shapira (Ed.), *Organizational decision-making.* New York: Cambridge University Press.

Ortony, A. (1979). *Metaphor and thought.* Cambridge, UK: Cambridge University Press.

Oxford Minidictionary. (1981). New York: Oxford University Press.

Pal, L. (1995). Competing paradigms in policy discourse: The case of international human rights. *Policy Sciences, 18*(2), 185-207.

Pal, L. (1996, March). *Ideas in action: Methodological issues in interpreting policy discourse.* Paper presented to the Western Political Science Association Annual Conference, San Francisco.

Palumbo, D. J., & Calista, D. J. (Eds.). (1987). Symposium on Implementation. *Policy Studies Review, 7*(1), 91-232.

Palumbo, D. J., & Calista, D. J. (Eds.). (1990). *Implementation and the policy process.* New York: Greenwood.

Paris, D. C., & Reynolds, J. F. (1983). *The logic of policy inquiry.* New York: Longman.

Patton, C. V., & Sawicki, D. S. (1993). *Basic methods of policy analysis and planning.* Englewood Cliffs, NJ: Prentice Hall.

Peattie, L. (1968). Reflections of an advocate planner. *Journal of the American Institute of Planners, 34*(2), 80-88.

Peng, T. K., Peterson, M. F., & Shui, Y.-P. (1991). Quantitative methods in cross-national management research. *Journal of Organizational Behavior, 12,* 87-107.

Polanyi, M. (1966). *The tacit dimension.* New York: Anchor.

Polkinghorne, D. (1983). *Methodology for the human sciences.* Albany: SUNY Press.

Polkinghorne, D. (1988). *Narrative knowing and the human sciences.* Albany: SUNY Press.

Pressman, J., & Wildavsky, A. (1984). *Implementation* (3rd ed.). Berkeley: University of California Press.

Prottas, J. M. (1979). *People-processing*. Lexington, MA: D.C. Heath.

Rabinow, P., & Sullivan, W. M. (Eds.). (1979). *Interpretive social science*. Berkeley: University of California Press.

Raelin, J. A. (1986). *The clash of cultures*. Boston: Harvard Business School Press.

Rein, M. (1976). *Social science and social policy*. New York: Penguin.

Rein, M. (1983a). Action frames and problem setting. In M. Rein (Ed.), *From policy to practice* (pp. 221-234). London: Macmillan.

Rein, M. (1983b). Value-critical policy analysis. In D. Callahan & B. Jennings (Eds.), *Ethics, the social sciences, and policy analysis*. New York: Plenum.

Rein, M., & Schon, D. A. (1977). Problem setting in policy research. In C. Weiss (Ed.), *Using social research in policy making*. Lexington, MA: Lexington Books.

Ricoeur, P. (1971). The model of the text: Meaningful action considered as text. *Social Research, 38*, 529-562.

Riessman, C. K. (1993). *Narrative analysis*. Newbury Park, CA: Sage.

Robertson, O. (1980). *American myth, American reality*. New York: Hill & Wang.

Roe, E. (1994). *Narrative policy analysis*. Durham, NC: Duke University Press.

Rorty, R. (1979). *Philosophy and the mirror of nature*. Princeton, NJ: Princeton University Press.

Rosenhan, D., Frederick, F., & Burrowes, A. (1968). Preaching and practicing. *Child Development, 39*, 291-301.

Ruderman, R. S. (1997). Aristotle and the recovery of political judgment. *American Political Science Review, 91*(2), 409-420.

Sapolsky, H. (1972). *The Polaris system development*. Cambridge: Harvard University Press.

Schein, E. H. (1985). *Organizational culture and leadership*. San Francisco: Jossey-Bass.

Schmidt, M. R. (1993). Grout: Alternative kinds of knowledge and why they are ignored. *Public Administration Review, 53*(6), 525-530.

Schneider, H., & Ingram, A. (1993). Social construction of target populations. *American Political Science Review, 87*, 334-347.

Schon, D. A. (1979). Generative metaphor. In A. Ortony (Ed.), *Metaphor and thought* (pp. 254-283). New York: Cambridge University Press.

Schon, D. A., & Rein, M. (1994). *Frame reflection*. New York: Basic Books.

Schram, S. F., & Neisser, P. T. (Eds.). (1997). *Tales of the state*. New York: Rowman & Littlefield.

Schutz, A. (1962). Collected Papers (Vol. 1). In M. Natanson (Ed.), *The hague*. The Netherlands: Martinus Nijhoff.

Schutz, A. (1967). *The phenomenology of the social world*. Evanston, IL: Northwestern University Press.

Sclove, R. E. (1989, June/July). *The nuts and bolts of democracy*. Paper delivered at the 5th Biennial International Conference of the Society for Philosophy and Technology, Bordeaux, France.

Smircich, L. (1995). Writing organizational tales: Reflections on 3 books on organizational culture. *Organization Science, 6*(2), 232-237.

Smith, S. (1972). Not waving but drowning. In H. Gardner (Ed.), *The new Oxford book of English verse 1250-1950*. Oxford, UK: Clarendon.

Spradley, J. P., & McCurdy, D. W. (1972). *The cultural experience*. Palo Alto: Science Research Associates, Inc.

Stone, D. A. (1988). *Policy paradox and political reason*. Glenview, IL: Scott, Foresman.

Taylor, C. (1971). Interpretation and the sciences of man. *Review of Metaphysics, 25,* 3-51.

Teuber, A. (1987). *Original intent.* Unpublished manuscript.

Throgmorton, J. A. (1991). The rhetorics of policy analysis. *Policy Sciences, 24,* 153-179.

Throgmorton, J. A. (1993). Survey research as rhetorical trope. In F. Fischer & J. Forester (Eds.), *The argumentative turn in policy analysis and planning.* Durham, NC: Duke University Press.

Tierney, W. G., & Lincoln, Y. S. (Eds.). (1997). *Representation and the text.* Albany: SUNY Press.

Torgerson, D. (1985). Contextual orientation in policy analysis. *Policy Sciences, 18,* 241-261.

Torgerson, D. (1986a). Between knowledge and politics. *Policy Sciences, 19,* 33-59.

Torgerson, D. (Ed). (1986b). Interpretive policy inquiry. *Policy Sciences, 19,* 307-405.

Trice, H. M., & Beyer, J. M. (1993). *The culture of work organizations.* Englewood Cliffs, NJ: Prentice Hall.

Tuan, Y-F. (1977). *Space and place.* Minneapolis: University of Minnesota Press.

Turner, B. A. (Ed.). (1990). *Organizational symbolism.* New York: Aldine de Gruyter.

Vale, L. J. (1998, Spring). Empathological places: Remarks on receiving the Rapkin award. *DUSP@MIT.now,* 33-34.

van Eeten, M. J. G. (1997). Policy narratives about flooding and dike improvement. *Beleid & Maatschappij 1,* 55-56.

Van Maanen, J. (1986). *Tales of the field.* Chicago: University of Chicago Press.

Van Maanen, J. (1995). *Representation in ethnography.* Thousand Oaks, CA: Sage.

Van Maanen, J. (1996). Commentary: On the matter of voice. *Journal of Management Inquiry, 5*(4), 375-381.

Vickers, Sir G. (1973). *Making institutions work.* London: Associated Business Programmes.

Wagenaar, H. (1997). Policy as fiction: Narrative and its place in policy practice. *Beleid & Maatschappij 1,* 55.

Waldo, D. (1968). *The novelist on organization and administration.* Berkeley: Institute of Governmental Studies, University of California, Berkeley.

Weatherley, R. (1979). *Reforming special education.* Cambridge: MIT Press.

Westerlund, G., & Sjostrand, S.-E. (1979). *Organizational myths.* New York: Harper & Row.

White, H. (1981). The narrativization of real events. In W. J. T. Mitchell (Ed.), *On narrative* (pp. 249-254). Chicago: University of Chicago Press.

Whyte, W. F. (1955). *Street corner society.* Chicago: University of Chicago Press. (Original work published 1943)

Whyte, W. F. (1984). *Learning from the field.* Beverly Hills, CA: Sage.

Wynne, B. (1992). Sheep farming after Chernobyl. In B. Lewenstein (Ed.), *When science meets the public.* Washington, DC: American Association for the Advancement of Science.

Yanow, D. (1985). *Government regulation of academic research: Recombinant DNA and Harvard University (A, B, and C)* (#9-380-517, revised January). Cambridge, MA: Harvard University, Institute for Educational Management.

Yanow, D. (1993). The communication of policy meanings: Implementation as interpretation and text. *Policy Sciences, 26*(1), 41-61.

Yanow, D. (Ed.). (1995a). Policy interpretations. [Special Issue]. *Policy Sciences, 28*(2).

Yanow, D. (1995b). Built space as story: The policy stories that buildings tell. *Policy Studies Journal, 23*(3), 407-422.

Yanow, D. (1996a). American ethnogenesis and public administration. *Administration & Society, 27*(4), 483-509.

Yanow, D. (1996b). *How does a policy mean? Interpreting policy and organizational actions.* Washington, DC: Georgetown University Press.

Yanow, D. (1997). Passionate humility in interpretive policy and administrative analysis. [Special Issue on "Interpretive and cultural theories in administration," Jon Jun (Ed.).] *Administrative Theory and Praxis, 19*(2), 171-177.

Yanow, D. (1998a). American ethnogenesis and the 1990 U.S. census. In C. Greenhouse (Ed.), *Democracy and difference.* Albany: SUNY Press.

Yanow, D. (1998b). *Doing American race/ethnicity: Ethnogenesis in policy and administrative practices.* Manuscript under review.

Yanow, D. (1998c). Space stories; Or, studying museum buildings as organizational spaces, while reflecting on interpretive methods and their narration. *Journal of Management Inquiry, 7*(3), 215-239.

Yanow, D. (in press). Public policies as identity stories: American race-ethnic discourse. In T. Abma (Ed.), *Telling tales: On narrative and evaluation: Vol. 6. Advances in Program Evaluation.* Greenwich, CT: JAI.

ABOUT THE AUTHOR

Dvora Yanow is Professor in the Department of Public Administration at California State University, Hayward, where she teaches in the public policy and organizational studies areas. Her research interests include interpretive approaches to policy analysis (most recently of American uses of "race" and "ethnicity"), cultural analyses of organizations (including the analysis of organizational metaphors and of built space, looking currently at museums and synagogues), and the history of ideas in the philosophy of social science (especially interpretive and feminist theories). She is the author of *How Does a Policy Mean? Interpreting Policy and Organizational Actions* (1996) and coauthor of "Culture and organizational learning" (*Journal of Management Inquiry,* 1993), as well as other articles in public policy, public administration, and organizational studies journals. She lives a methodically chaotic life among many plants and stacks of papers and music.

Qualitative Research Methods

Series Editor
JOHN VAN MAANEN
Massachusetts Institute of Technology

Associate Editors:
Peter K. Manning, *Michigan State University*
& Marc L. Miller, *University of Washington*

Other volumes in this series listed on outside back cover

CPSIA information can be obtained
at www.ICGtesting.com
Printed in the USA
FFOW03n0327050817
38509FF

9 780761 908272